What Next?

What Next?

Educational Innovation and Philadelphia's School of the Future

Mary Cullinane and Frederick M. Hess
Editors

HARVARD EDUCATION PRESS
CAMBRIDGE, MASSACHUSETTS

Library of Congress Control Number 2009942746

Paperback ISBN 978-1-934742-44-0
Library Edition ISBN 978-1-934742-45-7

Published by Harvard Education Press,
an imprint of the Harvard Education Publishing Group

Harvard Education Press
8 Story Street
Cambridge, MA 02138

Cover Design: Perry Lubin

The typefaces used in this book are Minion and Helvetical Neue

The Educational Innovations Series

The *Educational Innovations* series explores a wide range of current school reform efforts. Individual volumes examine entrepreneurial efforts and unorthodox approaches, highlighting reforms that have met with success and strategies that have attracted widespread attention. The series aims to disrupt the status quo and inject new ideas into contemporary education debates.

Series edited by Frederick M. Hess

Other books in this series:
Bringing School Reform to Scale
by Heather Zavadsky

Contents

1

School of the Future and High School Redesign

Frederick M. Hess, Thomas Gift,
and Mary Cullinane

WHEN IT OPENED IN West Philadelphia in fall 2006, School of the Future (SOF) was the result of a highly unusual collaboration between the School District of Philadelphia—then led by CEO Paul Vallas—and the Microsoft Corporation. A $63 million public high school built for a 750-member student body, SOF was designed to fundamentally reshape the high school experience through new models for teaching and learning. It implemented innovative solutions in the areas of data and curriculum management, content development and distribution, virtual simulations and mentoring, and personalized instruction. The school quickly gained stature as a bold attempt at high school redesign, and its partnership with the world's most renowned technology company made it the subject of widespread attention.

SOF is not the first major effort at high school redesign, but it does provide a fresh lens through which to explore how such an ambitious process actually unfolds on the ground and what it means for future efforts at replication. National Public Radio referred to the school as "the next big thing," *Education Week* has described it as "a new high-tech school [that is] strutting its stuff," and NBC News has said that it offers a "next-generation education."

Education officials from more than fifty countries have visited SOF, and as a result of its work in Philadelphia, Microsoft created the Innovative Schools Program, which uses the 6I Development Process. It is now being used by organizations in more than fifteen countries around the world.

SOF is particularly noteworthy because of its declared intent to craft a reproducible and scalable design. The school was based on a framework for decision making that became known as the "6Is": introspection, investigation, inclusion, innovation, implementation, and, again, introspection. While not unique to school creation, the process was meant to be a model for helping both school systems and education providers create quality learning environments equal to twenty-first-century challenges. Moreover, the school is funded in the same way and at the same level as other Philadelphia public high schools. It was designed in accordance with the governance and accountability requirements of the school district and the Commonwealth of Pennsylvania, and as a neighborhood high school without admission standards.

The aim of this volume is to understand the first three years of SOF (2006–2009) more fully and to discover what it can teach about high school redesign, public-private partnerships, and the use of technology in school reform. While it is too early to evaluate the school in a summative fashion, there is much to be learned from a formative assessment of its genesis, design, execution, and implementation. Indeed, SOF offers a provocative window into high school redesign and new school creation within an urban district. In the No Child Left Behind era, and at a time when U.S. Secretary of Education Arne Duncan has called for shuttering and then reopening or replacing thousands of schools a year across the country, this closely drawn account illustrates the opportunities and the challenges that reformers can anticipate.

It should be noted that this volume would not have been feasible without Microsoft's and SOF's involvement. Their roles were vital in ensuring that the contributors had the access and cooperation essential to conduct an in-depth examination. That very relationship, of course, means that it would be foolhardy to attempt to present findings as an independent evaluation. Instead, the objective is to learn more about how teaching, learning, leadership, and familial and community engagement have unfolded at SOF and how successful reforms can be delivered at scale.

This book is first and foremost a tale of high school redesign and new school creation. Technology is a crucial element of SOF and was integral to its design, but the school was driven more by Microsoft's people and engineering process than by technology. This account presumes that technology is one part of the SOF narrative, but not that it is the main story or that technology is by itself transformative. In the following chapters, a select group of researchers, educators, and practitioners offer bold and insightful takes on when and how technology-based school redesign leads to improved teaching and learning, when it does not, and what this means in terms of dramatically improving the American high school.

WHAT IS SCHOOL OF THE FUTURE?

Although it was never the main focus of the endeavor, SOF was designed to incorporate technology into every aspect of the teaching and learning process. The facilities include a five-hundred-seat auditorium, wireless Internet access throughout the building, and online digital smart boards through which teachers can access needed information. Every classroom is wired for DVDs, video projects, and video conferencing. The school was also designed to be energy efficient and environmentally friendly, garnering the third-highest level in the Leadership in Energy Environmental Design rating system of the U.S. Green Building Council.

In SOF's inaugural year, the 170-member freshman class was selected from a lottery that attracted more than 1,500 applicants. Seventy-five percent of the learners (students) in the initial cohort were chosen from the surrounding West Philadelphia neighborhood, while the remaining 25 percent came from across the city. The school has grown each year to encompass one additional grade. By the time the school is fully populated, it will enroll 750 learners in grades nine through twelve. The class of 2010 (the first freshman cohort) is 95 percent African American, and 85 percent of learners come from low-income families. About 10 percent of the learners require special education services.

The first achievement results for learners attending School of the Future were available in fall 2009. Because Pennsylvania tests its high school students during grade eleven, and because SOF had no eleventh graders during its first two years of operation (2006–2007 and 2007–2008)—it started by enrolling just ninth graders and then added one new grade level each year—the first cohort of SOF eleventh graders took the Pennsylvania state test in spring 2009. Of course, those results offer merely a snapshot of the performance of SOF's first cohort at one point in time and cannot provide any insight into how well those learners are faring relative to their peers in other Philadelphia schools. Nor will such snapshot assessments shed much light, especially in their first few years, on the performance of SOF. The first evaluation of SOF performance is anticipated in late 2010. It is being conducted currently by Steven Gross, a professor of educational administration at Temple University.

SOF is operated by the School District of Philadelphia, the eighth-largest in the country by student enrollment. The district's 2008 operating budget was $2.2 billion for 167,000 students, or about $11,490 per pupil. Its overall student population is 62 percent African American, 17 percent Hispanic, and 13 percent white. The district operates 177 elementary schools, 28 middle schools, and 60 high schools, with 10,000 teachers and 25,000 employees. There are also 38 privately managed district schools and 61 charter schools. On the 2007–2008 Pennsylvania System of School Assessment, 45 percent of students scored "advanced" or "proficient" in reading, and 49 percent did so in math. In reading, 33 percent of students scored "below basic," while 31 percent were at the same level in math.

TECHNOLOGY HAS FREQUENTLY BEEN PITCHED AS A SOLUTION

In the past few years, grand claims have been made for technology's ability to revolutionize teaching and learning. In the much-discussed 2008 volume, *Disrupting Class: How Disruptive Innovation Will Change the Way the World Learns,* Clayton Christensen, a professor at Harvard Business School, and his coauthors argue that technology-based forces of "disruptive innovation" have clustered around public education and will eventually upend the way students learn. In particular, they say, technology will undercut the current model of standardization in education, thus opening the floodgates for customized, student-centered learning poised to alter the traditional classroom experience dramatically.[1]

Similarly, in the 2009 book *Liberating Learning: Technology, Politics, and the Future of American Education,* Terry Moe, a senior fellow at Stanford's Hoover Institution, and John Chubb, cofounder of Edison Learning, map out a dynamic vision of the nation's educational future. More specifically, they predict that innovations will eventually revamp schools to the great benefit of the nation's children—especially as it pits technology against entrenched special interests that perpetuate the educational status quo. "Technology promises to let a thousand flowers bloom," they declare. "The possibilities are exciting—and astounding."[2]

In some ways, however, these optimistic visions run counter to a body of evidence suggesting that when it comes to improving educational results, technology has thus far not met expectations. Journalist Todd Oppenheimer points out in *The Flickering Mind* that the potential of technology has persistently gone unreached, and that smart boards, diagnostic software, computers, and the Internet are simply a series of expensive baubles shoveled into otherwise unchanged schools and classrooms. As Oppenheimer reflects, "The computer industry has managed to survive on such a plethora of hype, habituating all of us to accept such a string of unfulfilled promises that we've long since lost the ability to see what new technological inventions really can and cannot do."[3] In 2007, the National Center for Education Evaluation and Regional Assistance released the results of a five-year, congressionally mandated study on the effectiveness of learning technology in K–12 classrooms. Employing data from thirty-three school districts and 132 schools, it found that "test scores were not significantly higher in classrooms using the reading and mathematics software products than those in control classrooms." For each of the four groups of products—which spanned first-grade early reading, fourth-grade reading comprehension, sixth-grade pre-algebra, and ninth-grade algebra—the evaluation found no clear differences in student achievement between the classrooms that used the technology products and those that did not.[4]

In 2003, the Institute of Education Sciences also published the comprehensive meta-analysis, *A Retrospective on Twenty Years of Education Technology Policy,* which surveyed twenty years of key policy reports addressing the challenges and opportunities involved in integrating technology into K–12 education. In summarizing these documents, the analysis noted that "what begins to surface is a widening gap between the promise and potential of technology and the ways in which technology actually gains traction in school settings."[5] From both supportive and critical writings, a clear message can be drawn: technology alone is not the answer.

A BIT OF HISTORY

Recent attempts to integrate technology into the K–12 classroom—SOF being a prominent example—are hardly the first such efforts. The first modern large-scale partnership between a school district and a major corporation to redesign schools through technology was the Apple Computers of Tomorrow (ACOT) project. ACOT was implemented in 1985 in two classrooms—one in Eugene, Oregon, and one in Blue Earth, Minnesota. Apple, then a young upstart, supplied computers and training for the teachers, while the school districts provided staffing and made physical modifications to the classrooms. The goal was to offer students constant access to computers and other digital technologies that they could integrate into all aspects of the learning process. In ACOT's second year, five new sites were added in four other states.

Before long, ACOT began to receive requests for information from other educators and the press. Visitors from South America and the U.S.S.R. toured the campuses. ACOT was profiled in *USA Today,* the *New York Times, Business Week,* and the *Boston Globe,* and was featured on NBC's

Nightly News.[6] From the beginning, ACOT teachers were required to report to project staff with observations about their experiences. In addition to weekly reports from each site, teachers sent monthly audio-taped journals in which they explained how they conducted instruction in their classrooms and the difficulties and successes they encountered.

By 1989, researchers from an array of institutions began to collect data in ACOT locales. Between 1991 and 1993, ACOT representatives made presentations to the U.S. Department of Education Goals Committee, the National Governors Association, the Education Commission of the States, the National Center for Education and the Economy, and the Federal Communications Commission. Despite its early successes and some positive evaluations, ACOT largely failed to deliver on early hopes for transformational change.[7] As Jan Hawkins, a former education professor at Harvard, observed,

> The tacit and achingly optimistic American belief that wonderful technologies will make things better has run into rough water. The efforts to engineer broad changes in education through designing the best materials, technologies, and programs have proved disappointing in many cases. It has proved disappointing in the general strategy beyond the particular technologies involved.[8]

Ultimately, what ACOT and more recent experiences indicate is how important the human factor is and how much implementation, organization, policy, and practice matter in determining whether new technologies deliver on their vast promise.

THE DESIGN AND LAUNCH OF SCHOOL OF THE FUTURE

The creators of School of the Future were aware of the challenges that had confronted school redesign efforts that attempted to sensibly employ technology. Moreover, they were aware that launching a redesign effort under the auspices of the Philadelphia School District—rather than as a more autonomous entity such as a charter school—would pose its own set of challenges. Nonetheless, they decided to pursue this course. The genesis of SOF began with an initial meeting between the CEO of the School District of Philadelphia and the general manager of Microsoft Education, Anthony Salcito. In this meeting, they discussed the challenges of high school redesign and their respective interest in addressing the problem. At the time, Philadelphia had recently been taken over by the state and a new school governance body had been implemented. The School Reform Commission represented a belief that the former school leadership had not been able to address the needs of children in Philadelphia and could no longer be entrusted with that role. Budget constraints, low morale, teacher shortages, high crime rates, and significant truancy were plaguing the district. CEO Paul Vallas was hired on a platform of reform and rebuilding. He believed strongly in multiple pathways to success and was interested in public and private partnerships.

Microsoft at the time was considering adding to its corporate campus a demonstration site focused on innovation in education. While current displays of the Home of the Future and the Information Worker Center provided insight into future lifestyles, the company lacked the ability to demonstrate how technology could affect the teaching and learning process. Salcito, however, felt strongly that Microsoft had the opportunity to do more. After discussions with and consideration from Microsoft's senior leadership, it was agreed that Microsoft would partner with the School District of Philadelphia to build a high school from the ground up. Microsoft communicated their desire for this effort to reflect three specific principles:

1. *Scalable.* The organization would need to address common constraints and challenges in a way that allowed other public school entities to look to it as a model for replication.
2. *Significant.* The organization should reside in an environment presented with significant social and economic challenges, therefore providing an example and hope for the most underserved populations.
3. *Sustainable.* Microsoft's commitment would be mostly human capital. Traditional school budgets would be allocated by the district and Microsoft would make significant contributions of employees, research, and partner support to the organization.

With these principles in mind, an agreement was reached to build a school capable of addressing the needs of twenty-first-century students, leveraging technology in appropriate ways but focusing on holistic reform. Many districts and others have asked, Why Philadelphia? While the Philadelphia school district's ability to agree to each of these principles is one element of a response to that question, a more significant answer is because they asked.

From the beginning, the development team worked on the operating principle, "learning first, technology later." While initial participants were skeptical, given the players involved, the authenticity of this principle quickly became apparent. Microsoft's project leader Mary Cullinane, a former educator, along with Ellen Savitz, the school district's chief development officer, focused the group on a broad range of introspection. People development, instructional redesign, organizational effectiveness, leadership, and facility design were investigated at length. Discussions of technology and software were minimal at first and treated as tactics rather than objectives. People received the greatest attention. Necessary competencies were identified for those who participated in the design process. Self-critical individuals with intellectual horsepower who were also able to deal with ambiguity and learn on the fly were recruited. Practitioners who were used to working with little engagement with others were brought together to debate and identify the mission and vision of the organization. Ideas were sought from both international experts and members of the local community. The broad range of participants presented both challenges and rewards.

Fundamental to the school's development was the leadership of both Microsoft and the school district. Paul Vallas and School Reform Commission chair James Nevels strongly believed in the work and its participants. They saw the effort as an opportunity to demonstrate to the world Philadelphia's commitment to improvement and innovation. Anthony Salcito and Linda Zecher of Microsoft also understood the importance of the work and supported the holistic approach being taken. While technology and software were not going to be a driving factor and while the environment chosen had a greater chance of failure than success, both believed the decision to work within the school district's confines represented the question that needed to be answered. This executive leadership proved critical in the early stages of development. Vallas and Nevels were called upon numerous times to address typical challenges encountered in urban redesign. Political considerations, internal supports, and community inclusion all required the backing of strong leadership. Both district leaders made it clear the successful opening of the school was a priority.

Many would consider the simple fact of opening of SOF a tremendous success worthy of replication. However, to end the story there would be inappropriate. In 2006, SOF opened its doors to great accolades and attention. What had been created and the possibilities it presented were refreshing. West Philadelphia, an area lacking examples of promise, quickly became a center of attention. The school's initial year, while challenging in some ways, was yielding positive trends in attendance and discipline. Yet changes in district leadership soon began to affect the school's ability to thrive. The departure of the CEO, chief academic officer, chief development officer, chief information officer, chief financial officer and chairman of the School Reform Commission all occurred within the first year of the school's operation. This perfect storm created a void that could not have been anticipated and its effects were to be felt.

Other factors besides the changes in leadership affected the experience at SOF. In keeping with the three principles of design, the school's governance model was typical of the district. While innovative hiring practices were implemented at large, a small percentage of traditional placements occurred at the school. Systemic budgeting practices created constant tension when trying to appropriate funds differently. Necessary district mandates, applicable and appropriate for the system, created an unnecessary workload and requirements at SOF. Regional leadership diluted effective communication between the district and the school, creating a lack of understanding and appreciation for all parties involved. While these challenges in themselves seem somewhat insignificant, collectively, given that the organization was in its infancy, they were daunting.

Challenges took many forms. The grading system deployed at SOF did not align with the fields used by the district's grading system. The professional development topics necessary for the staff did not align with the professional development days that were required by the district. The individuals at the district offices responsible for ordering textbooks did not recognize that SOF was not using textbooks, and therefore initially insisted on placing an order. Each of these incidents does not seem insurmountable, yet the time and energy required to address these challenges represented an inefficient use of time and resource.

In spite of these circumstances, one must look at SOF as an organization that has weathered tremendous strife, and we must consider what elements of its design have allowed this to occur. Clearly, being in its infancy during a time of great unrest was its greatest challenge. Without the necessary history, systemic culture, and instructional knowledge that are made possible only by time, SOF faced seemingly insurmountable odds.

TWO DECADES OF HIGH SCHOOL REDESIGN

SOF is an exemplar of a class of school design that is generally termed whole-school reform (also known as comprehensive school reform). Whole-school reform seeks to change all elements of a school's operating environment in accord with, as RAND's Brent Keltner noted more than a decade ago, "a central, guiding vision."[9]

In 1997, states and districts around the country embraced whole-school reform, largely in response to the Comprehensive School Reform Demonstration program, which made $150 million in federal funds available to school districts.[10] Nearly three thousand schools received awards of at least $50,000 to implement whole-school models or to develop research-based reforms.[11] Many of the programs receiving attention in the whole-school reform movement were initiated by New American Schools (NAS). NAS was formed in 1991 as the New American School Development Corporation, but it evolved into a program that offered training and implementation assistance to support whole-school models.[12]

The results of the whole-school movement were generally viewed as a disappointment. In 1998, the RAND Corporation studied schools that were implementing whole-school reforms and found that only about half of them were implementing even the core elements of their design models.[13] In addition, a 1999 study by the American Institutes for Research found that only three out of the twenty-four whole-school reform models studied presented strong evidence that they raised student achievement.[14] NAS also admitted in a 1999 report that even when schools have tried to implement whole-school reform, "some schools have not achieved the results they expected, and a few have not experienced any improvement after adopting a design."[15]

A similar scenario played out in the "small high school" movement that has dominated high school reform for much of the past decade. A series of promising small-scale efforts (influentially profiled by Tom Toch in *High Schools on a Human Scale*), with the ardent and expansive support of the Bill & Melinda Gates Foundation, gave rise to a wave of efforts to "break up" big high schools and replace them with many more intimate schools.[16] From 2000 to 2006, the foundation gave grants to more than two thousand high schools, eight hundred of which were existing schools attempting to partition themselves into several smaller ones.[17]

The mantra of "rigor, relevance, and relationships" drove billions of dollars in philanthropic and district spending. The results, however, were mixed at best. In a 2007 study, Barbara Schneider, Adam Wyse, and Venessa Keesler found that students in large schools achieved at levels on standardized math exams comparable to students at small schools, although students at small schools were more likely to apply to college and to four-year institutions.[18] Valerie Lee and Julia Smith identified in a 2007 report that high schools can be *too* small, that students were not learning as effectively in schools with too few students.[19] In 2000, Linda Darling-Hammond, Peter Ross, and Michael Milliken reviewed more than one hundred studies and found that smaller high schools were associated with only modestly enhanced academic achievement.[20] The Gates Foundation eventually shifted its focus away from small high schools, and the movement lost steam.

Beyond the particulars of comprehensive reform or small school reform, it is noteworthy that much of what passes for high school redesign is not particularly revelatory. A large amount of existing research merely offers broad encomiums on the need for standards, capacity-building, alignment, and the like. A vivid exhibition is David Marsh and Judy Codding's 1998 *The New American High School,* which hardly goes out on a limb in asserting that schools should

> provide a safe, clean environment for everyone; Decide on clear, high standards for student performance; . . . Develop a school climate and organization that produces strong, personal support for each student; . . . Provide strong support for every staff member to acquire the professional skill and knowledge needed to succeed in his or her job . . . [and] Develop a school leadership style that is inclusive, making everyone, including staff, students, and parents, feel that they are welcome participants in the drive to improve results.[21]

In short, high school reform has frequently echoed the platitudes, truisms, and demands for "more, better" strategies that characterize school reform more generally.

TECHNOLOGY-BASED SCHOOL REDESIGN

SOF is one of many ongoing efforts to support high school redesign with technology, making its experiences instructive and germane to an array of schools and districts facing or contemplating similar initiatives. What is unique in this case is not that SOF is wrestling with thorny educational challenges, but that it has thrown open its hatch to a collection of scholars and analysts so they can document and consider the experiences and lessons of the school.

One of the most well-known high-tech redesign efforts is High Tech High in San Diego, which was founded in 2000 by a coalition of San Diego educators and business leaders as a single charter high school. Now comprised of six schools— three high schools, two middle schools, and one elementary—High Tech High enrolls about 2,500 students and has roughly three hundred employees.[22] The school's facilities were designed to support key program elements, such as team teaching, integrated curriculum, project-based learning, community-based internships, frequent student presentations, and exhibitions.[23] To date, the results appear impressive, with 100 percent of graduates admitted to college. In 2006, the school was also the nation's first charter school authorized to credential its own teachers, essentially becoming its own college of education.

Another prominent example of technology-based redesign is the similarly named High Tech High School, a suburban district school in North Bergen, New Jersey. Opened in 1991, High Tech High School is a school of choice that offers challenging academics in a technology-based environment. Students can enroll in four or more years of math, science, social studies, English, and technology. They also have the opportunity to participate in four years of a foreign language, including Japanese, Spanish, and French. Students major in one of four areas—information technologies, science technologies, business, and the arts—which are intended to enable students to foster original thinking, solve problems, effectively use resources, acquire collaboration skills, and develop flexibility in technology-rich settings.[24]

When it comes to scaling these types of individual high-tech school models, perhaps the best-known example is the New Technology Foundation (NTF). Established in 1999 as a 501(c)(3) nonprofit organization working to achieve national reform with schools aiming to emulate the Napa New Technology High School (NTHS), NTF's mission is "to reinvent teaching and learning for the twenty-first century by offering a proven model and a fully integrated suite of tools designed to facilitate the creation and management of a relevant and engaging twenty-first-century education."[25] In pursuing that goal, NTF provides support to the original NTHS in Napa and offers interested schools tools, materials, and training in the NTHS methodology.[26] Partnering with organizations like Adobe, Cisco Systems, the Bill & Melinda Gates Foundation, and Microsoft, the NTHS Network is currently comprised of forty schools across the United States that use the NTHS approach to technology.[27]

RESEARCH ON TECHNOLOGY AND SCHOOL REDESIGN

Several recent volumes have examined questions related to the integration of technology in classrooms—such as the extent to which technology improves or hinders student learning and whether technology can be used to complement or supplant traditional teaching approaches—but none has provided the kind of practical look at the challenges of combining high school redesign with technology that the contributors provide here.

One strand of research inquires into the landscape in which students and educators use technology to redesign schools. Volumes such as Victor Asal and Paul Harwood's *Educating the First Digital Generation: Educate Us* and Lesley Farmer's *Teen Girls and Technology: What's the Problem, What's the Solution?* provide background on the adoption of technology in schools, but they focus especially on macro trends and broad social phenomena rather than on the practical challenges of using technology to rethink learning or design schools.[28]

Another body of work evaluates the effectiveness of technology in K–12 schools, drawing normative conclusions about its impact on student performance. Such books as David Kritt and Lucian Winegar's *Education and Technology* and Marge Cambre and Mark Hawkes's *Toys, Tools, & Teachers* have considered the benefits and shortcomings of technology in the classroom at some length. However, the focus of these accounts has mostly been on how technology affects the quality of teaching and learning more broadly.[29]

The books most closely mirroring this volume are the studies of schools using technology, particularly Andrew Zucker's *Transforming Schools with Technology*, Mary Burns and K. Victoria Dimock's *Technology as a Catalyst for School Communities*, and Eileen Coppola's *Powering Up*.[30] Zucker's volume examines broad questions about the current and potential roles for technology in the classroom, such as enhancing teacher quality and improving performance measurements. Burns and Dimock chronicle the stories of three K–12 schools struggling to integrate technology into the classroom, focusing on how to improve professional development, ensure that educators have the necessary technical skills, and devise curricula for high-tech classrooms. Coppola provides an in-depth study of a school using computers, which considers how the policies, structure, and culture of a school can support efforts to implement learning-based technologies in the classroom. Each of these accounts is a useful complement to this volume.

KEY CHALLENGES FOR TECHNOLOGY-AIDED SCHOOL REDESIGN

Previous scholarship has suggested that efforts to pursue school redesign through technology confront a number of key challenges. One is context and the need to account for the environment in which school redesign takes place. Such distinctions include school size, achievement level, demographics, budgets, and community needs. As Decker Walker, an education professor at Stanford, has described,

> Neither powerful technology nor good ideas are enough to improve education. Success in using computers in education will come only as a result of the intelligent and artful orchestration of many details in the classroom . . . Educational programs are not machines, but they are complex social systems and making them work is at least as difficult as making machines work.[31]

A second challenge is that posed by assessment—particularly the need to collect appropriate data, use data to facilitate implementation, and monitor its use and impact. In particular, it is vital to explore high-tech assessment tools that can save teachers time, increase efficiency, and help educators diagnose student needs and track student progress far more efficiently. As Jan Hawkins has noted,

> Assessment procedures may appear to be a small and bothersome element of fundamentally reconceived education . . . [But] the kinds of representations and records that constitute the core of any assessment system fundamentally define the real stance toward knowledge that is in effect. Representations of student progress that are complex yet manageable are essential if

we are to create a system in which the pedagogy is not in tacit conflict with the accounting.[32]

A third challenge is that created by the need to scale and replicate success-ful ventures. It requires broad-scale commitment and cooperation among businesses, organizations, and schools, but cannot simply be a question of collaboration and best practices. Beyond that, there is a need to create eco-systems in which innovators can solve problems, adopt new solutions, and deliver them at scale in new ways that take advantage of new tools.

Fourth, making use of new schoolwide or classroom technologies requires sensible and appropriate professional development. Educators need instruc-tion both on using technology themselves and on teaching students to use it. As Jane David, director of the Bay Area Research Group, has argued,

> To help teachers incorporate technology in ways that support powerful in-struction requires an array of professional development experiences quite different from traditional workshops and how-to training sessions. Rather than focusing on technology per se, these requisite experiences must focus on changing pedagogical benefits and practices, with technology as a tool when appropriate. The crucial role of technology is to provide an impetus and an occasion for thinking differently about instructional practices.[33]

Fifth, design and integration pose a particular challenge. There is a need to reconfigure classrooms and schools so that they are suited to handle new types of technology, and not to simply append dynamic new gizmos to existing structures. Redesign and technology integration go hand in hand; simply inserting computers into otherwise unaltered classrooms is a recipe for disappointment.

Finally, there is a particular need for technology-reliant schools to learn and adapt, and to pursue continual evaluation and change to meet the de-mands of twenty-first-century schooling. Simply put, if SOF stays the same for the next decade without revisiting and rethinking its technology, cur-riculum, and practices, it will quickly become a "school of the past." The goal must not and cannot be change for the sake of change, but to continually seek out ways in which new tools and technology make it possible to meet pressing challenges in smarter or better ways.

THE VOLUME FROM HERE

The following chapters seek to answer two overarching questions. First, how was SOF created and what technologies, practices, and tools were built into the design? Second, how have these elements changed (or not changed) teaching, learning, and schooling? These questions will be addressed in the course of eight chapters and in some closing remarks by the editors.

In chapter 2, Jan Biros, associate vice president at Drexel University, considers SOF's design process and how it has played out. In particular, she examines the unique "project-based" curriculum at SOF and how Microsoft's 6I Development Process actually worked on the ground. In chapter 3, Doug Lynch, vice dean of the Graduate School of Education at the University of Pennsylvania, and his colleagues explain the technology of SOF and how it has been integrated into the classroom. He defines technology broadly to include not only the hardware and software, and also looks at issues related to governance, finance, and curriculum. Chapter 4 focuses on the role of school leadership. Coauthors Matthew Riggan, a researcher at the Consortium for Policy Research in Education at the University of Pennsylvania, and Margaret Goertz, a professor of education policy at the University of Pennsylvania, investigate the role of SOF's leaders—especially its chief learners (principals)—and how they have affected the culture and practice of the school. They place particular emphasis on how leadership style and turnover have affected SOF's orientation toward its founding principles.

Patrick McGuinn, associate professor of political science at Drew University, takes a close look at parental and community and engagement in chapter 5. Specifically, he points out a number of challenges that SOF has faced in promoting involvement with external stakeholders. In chapter 6, Dale Mezzacappa, a former education journalist at the *Philadelphia Inquirer*, takes a close look at educators and teaching. She discusses the hiring process for SOF educators (teachers) and their ability to adapt to and thrive within SOF's distinctive environment. In chapter 7, SOF faculty members collaborate to provide an insider's look at how teaching and learning unfold at the school when things are clicking. In chapter 8, coeditor Mary Cullinane, director of innovation and business development for the Microsoft Corporation, offers a first-person take on key lessons learned and reflects on the implications for high school redesign. She summarizes the ideas she feels are worth emulating from SOF and explains what reformers can build on going forward.

In chapter 9, Chester E. Finn Jr., president of the Thomas B. Fordham Foundation and a senior fellow at Stanford's Hoover Institution, offers a broader and more historical take on technology-driven reform and the promise of redesign efforts. Finn draws on two decades of personal experience to put the lessons learned in context. Finally, since Finn does an exemplary job of distilling key themes and lessons from two decades of experience, we close the volume by proffering a few words on what we have attempted to do here and why this kind of effort is so valuable, and a few words of reflection (and, hopefully, wisdom) for practitioners, policy makers, and would-be reformers going forward.[34]

2

Twixt the Cup and the Lip

From Design to Execution

Jan Biros

I WAS THRILLED WHEN I was asked to participate on the curriculum-planning committee for School of the Future in 2004. In the many years that I managed academic computing at Drexel University, I had myriad opportunities to work with the School District of Philadelphia on technology-integration projects, and I always looked forward to them. Although I was used to the sometimes wide disparity between the promise of educational technology and the realities of implementation, I went into the project with high hopes. After all, we were to have the guidance and assistance of Microsoft, the world's leading technology company.

The original conception of SOF came from Paul Vallas, the district's CEO, who had been recruited from Chicago to turn around the struggling Philadelphia school system. Vallas, who had been singled out by President Clinton as being responsible for raising test scores, improving relations with teachers, and increasing positive engagement with the community, saw SOF as the paradigm for a new kind of neighborhood high school. It was to be built by the School District of Philadelphia with the guidance, inspiration, and support of Microsoft. From the outset, Vallas and the project planners conceived of the school as a model for a local high school rather than as a magnet school with students selected by ability. The plan called for 75 percent of its

750 students to come from the surrounding West Philadelphia neighborhood and the remaining 25 percent to come from the rest of the district. Both groups of learners would be selected via a random lottery.

Microsoft sought to provide strong leadership for the curriculum committee and the entire project through one of their education specialists, Mary Cullinane. She was dedicated to managing all aspects of the project and was the major liaison among Microsoft, the school district, and the community. There was also strong central support from the chair of the School Reform Commission and two other senior regional administrators. Vallas convinced a recently retired school principal to return to the district to provide additional functional leadership. These individuals were deeply committed to the success of SOF and were especially qualified to do so. The curriculum-planning committee, of which I was a member, was responsible for creating the vision and blueprint for SOF. We were a group of approximately twenty professionals from the school district, universities, or educational agencies.

THE VISION

SOF entailed many levels of design, development, and implementation. The actual construction had major financial implications for a district fraught with funding deficits. The planners saw SOF as significantly more than a construction project, however. It was an opportunity to design a curriculum, a culture, and a community of learners using new tools and pedagogical approaches. It was an opportunity to alter public high school management and organization and challenge the reward system for both students and faculty. And it was an opportunity to rethink daily schedules, use of time in school, and all the accepted conformities repeated year after year in public education.

Our curriculum committee understood that making SOF a success would require broad thinking, creativity, and careful planning to erect a new model for public high school education. Complicating the process, however, were demographic issues presented by the local community. The students were to be primarily African Americans from families with social and economic challenges. Their neighborhood was deteriorating, and residents faced problems such as unemployment, single parenthood, and neighborhood crime. Educators at the school would likely face behavior and truancy issues, learning disabilities, and motivational problems.

Microsoft's role was not to build the school, but to offer professional expertise to guide and inform a "proof of concept" that could be replicated. Microsoft agreed to develop new tools and applications that would allow students to access learning materials using laptops and other personal digital devices. It also arranged to provide its own planning and management tools, affording new standards for technology implementation, accountability, and assessment.

It is important to note that technology was intended to facilitate rather than drive SOF. The primary objective was to stimulate high-quality, relevant education that would equip students for college. Technology would be at everyone's fingertips, and access to information would be ubiquitous. The curriculum would be project based and collaborative. Technology would support analysis, synthesis, and critical thinking about content and information. The plan was that the educators and learners would not use or need books. Their curricula, projects, assignments, assessments, and communication would be done exclusively online and on their laptops.

THE PLAN

One of the problems with utopian visions is that they tend to be short on specifics. While our curriculum committee concentrated on discussing broad issues, we did not discuss how SOF would relate to district policies and standards. We talked about the school as an independent entity and made our plans in isolation, without much regard for economic or political realities. For instance, we all agreed that students should be evaluated qualitatively without customary grades and standardized tests, but we did not consider how colleges would use these assessments to determine students' acceptance into their programs.

We were not naïve, but some of our assumptions were flawed. We conceived of SOF as an island unto itself, unique and unrelated to the district of which it was a part. Because Microsoft was providing guidance and Vallas was behind the project, our attitude seemed appropriate. Perhaps being overly idealistic, we felt that once SOF was established and successful, its best practices would be implemented throughout Philadelphia. However, we were also not clear what role, if any, Microsoft would play after the school opened. We knew there was no intention to have SOF function as a Microsoft school with ongoing mentoring and stewardship from the software giant. Microsoft was, rather, the catalyst and our guide. The problem is that we paid scant attention to how they would perform in that role.

We knew from the beginning that for any goal to be successful and to result in demonstrable, measurable results, there must be a well-established, documented plan that would keep everyone focused on the school's missions and requirements. Microsoft provided this for SOF through the 6I Development Process. The "I's" represent six broad steps: introspection, investigation, inclusion, innovation, implementation, and, again, introspection. The curriculum committee also agreed on several underlying principles as a foundation for their plans:

- Learning is primary and technology will follow
- Language and effective communication are paramount
- A lack of process impedes success
- Everyone should be comfortable not knowing
- Questions should be identified and raised first and answers will come

The 6Is were supposed to offer a mechanism to document and replicate the strategic process and to organize the thinking, activities, and products emerging throughout the project. Unfortunately, working within this framework at times felt more like an academic exercise than a productive process. Descriptions posted on the Microsoft Web site were impressive, but sometimes seemed vague and general.

Introspection

The introspection stage was meant to create a common language to describe the mission of SOF. This entailed bringing together stakeholders to brainstorm what the learning environment should look like. The first such session attracted nearly thirty educators from the school district, colleges and universities, and educational organizations. After much discussion, participants wrote a brief reflection on their image of SOF. The curriculum committee then spent a day creating the following six questions to address:

1. What are you trying to create?—Creating a common vision
2. Who are you creating it for?—Know your customer(s)
3. How will you organize your work?—Define scope
4. What process will discipline your effort?—Disciplined methodology
5. What factors are critical for success?—Establish a common language
6. What assets are required to support your critical success factors?—Less is more

While it was challenging to identify critical success factors—the key criteria that we would use to guide the planning process and frame assessment and evaluation—we eventually agreed on several goals and expectations:

- Be an involved and committed learning community
- Provide a proficient and inviting curriculum-driven setting
- Be a flexible and sustainable learning environment
- Promote cross-curriculum integration of research and development
- Have excellent professional leadership

It was at this time that our curriculum committee decided that SOF's mission statement would be "to create an environment where learning is continuous, relevant, and adaptable." In doing so, we hoped to promote an environment in which learning would be independent of time and place, and where the content, curriculum, and tools would be current and relevant. More important, we hoped that we could adapt our instruction to each individual's learning style, situation, and environment.

Investigation

Investigation was an opportunity to review research, identify best practices, and conduct a "SWOT" analysis—for strengths, weaknesses, opportunities, and threats—of proposed plans and ideas. Microsoft identified similar projects elsewhere, and several members of the committee made field trips to these sites. I was part of the group that visited the Irving Academy in the Independent School District of Irving, Texas. The school was an impressive, brand new, technology-centered high school with a technical and vocational curriculum. Students designed their course of study and were expected to be independent learners. They used laptops throughout the wireless building, and every nook and cranny was a space for learning and collaboration. It seemed that the students were engaged and energized by their learning. It was one of many proof-of-concept examples that led us to believe we could achieve our goals.

Inclusion

Our curriculum committee recognized that even though students who would attend SOF lived in the sixth-largest city in the country, many of them were isolated from the wealth of cultural resources that Philadelphia had to offer. Many had never seen the rich historical treasures just a few blocks away. Some had never been inside the country's first zoo, which was only a block away from their new school. Working with representatives of local universities, community organizations, and cultural groups, we proposed mentoring programs, on-site short courses, internships, and other opportunities that would enable students to venture out into their community and expand their learning and life experiences. In addition, we proposed that SOF educators should not be limited to the educators assigned to that school, but should also include parents, community leaders, and others.

Our curriculum committee also agreed that the school should be a resource for the entire neighborhood—not just for the students enrolled. We stipulated that SOF should be used beyond the normal 8:00 a.m. to 5:00 p.m., Monday through Friday schedule and should provide educational opportunities and support to adults in the neighborhood. We saw SOF as the venue where job-skills programs, computer classes, and exercise, health, and wellness programs would be offered to the community. Our vision was to provide a highly valued and appreciated resource for the whole neighborhood. No one at the time addressed the cost issues related to increased hours, however, or whether our vision was feasible or even practical.

Implementing and sustaining external partnerships—while desirable—is difficult. Partnerships often are dependent on one interested, committed individual who may or may not remain in their current position or have the authority and resources to implement plans. In addition, partnerships require coordination and nurturing from the school to keep all of them vital, valuable, and scalable. The competing priorities and responsibilities within organizations often relegate optional partnerships to the back burner or off the stove completely.

Innovation

True innovation in school reform is a challenge because the accepted models for educational operation and instructional delivery are so well established, locally and nationally, that they cannot easily be disregarded. Contemporary students may be educated using creative pedagogies and new technologies, they may be assessed in their innovative educational environment using alternate forms of evaluation and assessment, but the reality is that they will still be judged by historical standards that may or may not have been part of the innovative model. While our curriculum committee proposed and described a creative new learning environment, we did it without addressing the hard questions of how to make it relevant and workable.

Implementation

Planning for SOF involved imagining the school building as well as the curriculum. The building process was not within the purview of our curriculum committee. Nevertheless, the planners incorporated our suggestions into the building design. We received periodic reports on construction, interior plans and selections, and special features to be included. We wanted the building to be open, modular, and flexible, which would enable us to adapt it to evolving learning modalities and the creative and innovative learning activities we anticipated. The building was to be "green" and "Gold LEED certified," and would embrace and demonstrate many of the environmental and sustainable concepts our students would be learning about.[1]

Building a new school is a huge undertaking anywhere, but doing so in Philadelphia was particularly challenging. The city bureaucracy and political climate presented endless obstacles: budgetary constraints provided an ongoing challenge; permits and licenses involved a great deal of red tape and time, which caused delays; and Philadelphia's strong union presence further complicated the process. Despite every obstacle the city could throw at us, the building itself was a triumph, even if it was completed under the considerable pressure of the start of the school year.

While the building planners were developing their portion of the implementation, we focused on our key success factors. The 6I Development Process mandates that to maximize outcomes, assets must be in place to support the critical success factors. For us, one of the most dynamic was strong professional leadership. Part of our preparation for implementation was selecting those largely responsible for the project's success: the educators. These educators needed certain unique assets to succeed: they had to be proficient in designing and delivering curricula in a variety of ways; they had to be creative and self-directed in their approach to teaching; they needed to understand and use technology effectively in order to deliver content and facilitate inquiry; they needed to be committed to helping people, particularly students, learn and grow; and they needed to be flexible and adaptable. At the same time, the institution had to be sustainable and independent of any one person or group. The success of a venture like SOF cannot depend on one particular personality because if that person disappears, the institution must continue with new leadership and new personalities and not be threatened or derailed by the change.

The planners recognized this at the school level but did not appreciate it at the district level. Because the school was developed as a unique and separate entity, it was vulnerable to the absence of the few champions it had—Vallas left and the few champions SOF had had gone on to other opportunities. At the time, none of the change were being integrated into larger district plans for reform or strategic development. While education reform can take place in one entity—even as a grassroots experience that then becomes a model for the rest of the organization—most of the more successful projects are districtwide. District initiatives provide a broader base to support and sustain reforms, and more stakeholders are involved to implement plans. This was not the case in Philadelphia.

Our curriculum committee set out to make the process of selecting professional leadership as objective, competency based, and thorough as possible. Microsoft had a structured plan for interviewing and hiring new employees and ensuring quality, consistency, and objectivity in the process. Microsoft calls it the Loop, and they modified it for education and introduced it into the SOF hiring process. They based the Loop on a Competency Wheel, which identifies the skills required for specific positions and roles within the company. As adapted for the SOF project, it graphically represented the factors educators identified as requirements for successful performance in education: courage, an orientation to results, strategic skills, operating skills, individual excellence, and organizational skills. The Loop also identifies all of the major subskills that compose these larger skills, and it is used to evaluate the skills and competencies of applicants and shows how they line up. Our curriculum committee used it to select the SOF educators.[2]

The Loop process was intended to facilitate hiring the best faculty possible with objective consideration and enable us to recruit several new educators interested in SOF. Most of the applicants, however, were current district teachers looking for new assignments. As I participated in the interview process, I was not confident that many of the teachers I interviewed had the creativity, pedagogical skills, or the technical ability to deliver the vision we had discussed and designed.

We did launch a national search for a principal, whom we referred to as the chief learner to communicate the message that SOF would be a learning environment for everyone involved, and that everyone would be learning and growing together. The search yielded a wide variety of applicants with varying backgrounds and levels of experience. Finalists participated in the Loop process and had many rigorous interviews. The original plan called for filling the position in time for the school's opening; however, after discussions and recommendations from our committee, the planners decided that the chief learner should be hired a year before the school opened in order to become familiar with the district, to learn the details of what was planned and expected, and to participate in the selection of the teaching faculty.

Once the chief learner was hired, the curriculum committee met regularly with her to describe in more detail the specifics of the curriculum and approaches. The new chief learner, who appeared bright and creative, had spent the previous ten years as principal of an international school in Italy. Understanding our vision, she was committed to innovation and to students. She was an experienced educator and administrator eager to implement the vision the curriculum committee had conceived and planned. We discussed with her our models for student engagement with the Philadelphia Zoo, the West Park Cultural and Opportunity Center, and the two universities in the neighborhood.

SPREADING THE GOSPEL

Microsoft did an excellent job of using the Internet to promote the SOF project and disseminate materials and ideas to other educators. Microsoft's objective was not to sell anything but to truly have an impact on education in a positive, constructive way and to help educators prepare themselves, and their schools, districts, and communities, to educate children in the new century. In 2005, Microsoft hosted the School of the Future World Summit at its corporate headquarters in Redmond, Washington. Over two hundred educators from thirty countries heard about what was happening in Philadelphia and what other similar initiatives were accomplishing. These included lighthouse schools that were employing innovative teaching approaches and using technology effectively in many areas, and the summit was an important opportunity to learn from them and benefit from their experiences.

The event brought together people from education systems around the world that represented different levels of development and diverse challenges. All were connected, however, by their interest in education reform and technology integration. Microsoft committed to continue the conversation and excitement by sponsoring subsequent online summits. They also sponsored a summit at SOF when it opened.

FINAL STAGES

The construction of the building was initiated with a symbolic groundbreaking ceremony, complete with dignitaries. It was exciting—and a long time coming. It was also the first indication that something would actually materialize from all of our years of talking.

Once construction actually began, things seemed to move fairly smoothly. However, it was a three-year journey from conception to completion. On the evening of our opening day, a gala was held for those involved with the project, which included dignitaries from Microsoft, the City of Philadelphia, and the State of Pennsylvania. The event took place in the school, and people made many wonderful, inspirational, moving speeches full of hope, promise, and thanks. The white school building looked fantastic—like a jewel sitting on a knoll overlooking the nearby houses. It featured lots of windows and gentle curves and turns in its design. The spacious entrance led to a large open food court that was to serve as the cafeteria and a gathering place. The huge windows let in lots of light and made the beautiful grounds outside an integral part of the environment. The auditorium had two revolving platforms that could be rotated to create smaller classrooms, and then turned back again to expand the main space. The building was impressive and welcoming, and inviting enough to make students want to come to school and stay there. It was an immaculate, stunning, safe haven for its students—that would be a new experience for many of them.

Finally, on September 7, 2006, School of the Future opened. It was wonderful to see this idea that we had talked about for three years finally come to fruition. The reactions of the students and parents as they came into the school were wonderful—everyone was in awe of this special place that was created for them. The first year opened with one class of ninth graders. The plan called for an additional class to be added each year, enabling activity to ramp up slowly and deliberately while working out all the kinks.

REALITY SETS IN

The planners designed School of the Future as a completely wireless environment supporting ubiquitous access to information. Students were able to use their computers inside or outside the building. However, this vital part of the school's technology was unstable and unreliable. SOF had no books, as all content and learning tools were to be online and available through a learning management portal software designed by Microsoft. When they were not accessible it was a problem. There was no institutionalized "safety net," and it seemed like a great leap of faith—faith that these educators, amid so many new circumstances, would be able to develop curriculum almost on the fly and store and distribute it electronically.

The district networking staff had responsibility for the network, but they were not on site. When problems occurred, they were not fixed immediately. And all too often they were not fixed effectively. This issue went on for many months, put undue stress on both educators and learners, and wasted valuable teaching and learning time.

There was also the matter of student computer problems. Each learner at SOF received a laptop computer and was directed to take it home at night and bring it back to school in the morning. While SOF began the school day later than other schools and remained open during the critical period from 3:00 p.m. to 5:00 p.m., when many students had no one at home, we still had serious concerns for student safety as they carried valuable equipment through their tough neighborhood. The school also had to deal with a large population of laptop users who had marginal computer literacy. The academic model depended on students using their computers constantly, but few had experience using and caring for one. This led to constant technical problems with e-mail use, document storage, and information management.

Teaching and learning at SOF was further complicated by the many visitors who came to the school each day. Microsoft had promoted its project especially well, and there was pent-up demand from educators throughout the world to witness SOF firsthand. These visitors often disrupted the school routine, which had not yet had a chance to establish itself, and were a disturbance to the chief learner and faculty. The students, however, did love being at school. They came early and stayed late, and for many it was better to be at school than at home. They were protective of their new school, too. On the first Halloween after the school opened, the students came at night to "guard" the building so that no one would vandalize it.

THE FIRST YEAR

As the year progressed, I could see the many stresses, strains, and difficulties that SOF was experiencing. Faculty members struggled to implement the portal and the online learning. The portal application was simultaneously under development and in use, and it was never fully tested. When I visited more recently, faculty members were still having problems posting lessons to the portal. Given the school's curricular objectives, when the technology did not work, it was a major obstacle for the educators. For many educators this was an entirely new approach, and both the pedagogical and technical issues created a difficult situation for them.

In addition, the students themselves posed a challenge. While they loved their new school, they were still generally an underserved, at-risk group. Therefore, in the classroom there were management issues, learning problems, kids with difficulties at home, and a myriad of other problems. Most disappointing, however, was that the novelty of SOF began to wear off at the district level and our innovative jewel was in danger of becoming just another school. Toward the end of the first year, there was even a threat of not having enough money to provide computers for the incoming freshman class. We faced a real danger that the key component of the entire educational plan would be unattainable.

Perhaps inevitably, the school also ran into administrative problems. The chief learner was not familiar with the political and bureaucratic complexities of the district and was not able to navigate the troubled waters and advocate for her school. In addition, many of our original district champions and supporters began leaving the district for opportunities elsewhere. What little support the chief learner had had rapidly eroded. Even Paul Vallas ran into difficulties with the School Reform Commission over large budget deficits, and he eventually left to help the New Orleans school district rebuild after Hurricane Katrina. The hard realities of the School District of Philadelphia looked far stronger than our rosy vision of the future.

Despite everything, I knew that the chief learner was working vigorously to make the new approaches to evaluation and teaching work, and that she was committed to her learners and their success.

THE SECOND YEAR

When I recently visited SOF after almost two years away from it, I was surprised and pleased to see how beautiful it still is. It still looked like a jewel sitting on the hill. I met a sharp, personable Microsoft employee who works there every day to help educators use and integrate technology into their classes. I asked him if he is a resource also tapped by other schools. He indicated that despite his efforts to reach out to other schools and faculties in support of academic technology, he had not been successful. I also observed a project-based math class at the school. The educator was in his second year teaching at SOF. He was disappointed that there was none of the discussion and brainstorming that had taken place the previous year. He said that his first year at SOF was the most creative time he had experienced in his life.

SOF has now hired a full-time technology support person to maintain laptops and make sure everything works well (better later than not at all). Drexel was chosen to host the portal and the major administrative, e-mail, and academic applications used in the school, and SOF computers run on servers in the Drexel data center two miles away.

The two chief learners who initially led SOF have been replaced by someone who has been successful in the district for many years and who also was on the school's curriculum-planning committee. She is extremely competent and can navigate the system well. But even she is having a hard time getting the district office's attention about matters with which she needs help. She has returned to the conventional curriculum standards prescribed by the district, and the school has become more structured in an effort to quell disciplinary problems. A new district superintendent was hired in 2008; as of this writing, she has not yet visited SOF.

CONCLUSION

In retrospect, perhaps SOF educators should also have been brought on long before the school opened so they could have received intensive professional development and training on using the new technologies, such as creating digital learning objects and curricular materials, and on reengineering their curriculum and pedagogy for the new environment. Intensive, ongoing development opportunities could have been planned for them. I was at SOF on an in-service day when the faculty was hearing a presentation on leadership. Perhaps continued development on pedagogy and technology integration would have been more valuable.

Essayons

When we were in the planning process for SOF, Microsoft came up with a watchword for the project: *essayons*—meaning "let us try." It is the motto of the Army Corps of Engineers. It was appropriate for us and our building project, and it is even more appropriate today as we are in the sixth "I" phase, introspection. As we reflect on what we have accomplished at the school, it is easy to see where the shortfalls are and more difficult to see the tangible results we have achieved. We certainly have not changed education in Philadelphia. Because true reform is a journey, essayons is a good motto for us to keep in mind. It is critical for educators to remain committed to changing education into a relevant, adaptable, and sustainable learning experience.

One of the unfortunate conclusions I have reached from my experience with SOF is that the visions of education reformers must come to terms with the realities of modern urban school districts. Even given the Microsoft brand, there are many vested interests, political landmines, and budget constraints that must be addressed before we can really accomplish our inspirational goal. What I have learned is that we may not yet be ready for a revolutionary change. It may be that education and SOF are severely hindered by the entrenched realities of the past, and that true education reform will take longer than we wish.

3

Technology

The Importance of Stability

Doug Lynch, Kabeera McCorkle,
Michael Gottfried, and Dorothea Lasky

IN ECONOMICS, A PRODUCTION function describes the relationship between inputs and outputs. The primary purpose of this rubric is to show how combinations of inputs influence a specified output. Economists think of a "better" combination of inputs (one that leads to lower costs or better outcomes) as technological innovation. That is, technology is an innovation in the utilization of input resources. Through the technology of improved resource allocation (such as more capital versus more labor), a firm can alter its status quo production to increase efficiency.

Economists have applied this concept to the field of education, using inputs such as students, classrooms, teachers, and school resources, and outputs such as test performance, high school graduation, and college enrollment. As in the traditional production function, the education production function is used to gauge innovations in school resources as they affect educational outcomes. This technological innovation enables a school to allocate its resources more effectively and gain a competitive advantage in improving its students' results. Indeed, an innovating school can change the landscape of learning.

School of the Future styles itself as an innovator, with its tech-savvy focus and its partnership with Microsoft, which could also be a "technology" as we have defined it. If SOF does provide educational innovation and if SOF's approach is replicable, then an investigation of how the school functions is warranted. Delving into the specific processes of SOF can serve as a weathervane of increased efficiency in public education, within the constraints of the School District of Philadelphia.

Our strategy uses the metaphor of the production function as a way of framing a discussion about innovation in SOF. We looked at technology broadly defined (as innovation in the use of input resources), including students, governance, finance, curriculum, and educational learning tools and devices. We intentionally did not consider faculty or leadership, as other chapters in this volume are explicitly devoted to these areas. That said, there is no neat way to parse only certain inputs into a production function; faculty and leadership probably matter more than anything else. Even so, a look at other innovations in inputs is warranted. To be clear, this is not a formal analysis of the array of inputs and outputs into the production function at SOF but, rather, a simple discussion of some facets of innovation at the school, using the economic paradigm to frame the discussion.

To gather data, we interviewed learners, educators, and staff. We found our interviewees to be candid, helpful, and forthcoming in their replies. We also examined written documents about the school composed by the district, Microsoft, and SOF staff. We wanted to get a benchmark for the level of innovation within SOF and to "control" for the city effect, so we investigated three other Philadelphia schools: the Science Leadership Academy (a Philadelphia magnet school), Penn Charter (an independent Philadelphia school), and Pennsylvania Virtual High School (which is delivered by K12 Inc.).

It is paramount that we frame this discussion properly. The innovative approach that SOF sought to develop and implement has not yet been fully realized, due to leadership changes, school district oversight, and other unanticipated challenges. At the time of this writing, SOF is in many ways still in the developmental stage, working toward its vision under increasing constraints. SOF has admirably welcomed researchers into its process of development, demonstrating a real willingness to be reflective. Our chapter discusses innovation at SOF in the interest of informing the development of the school and future research, thus contributing to a larger national discussion about innovation in public schooling. What we aim to explore is the impact of introducing a technology, as we define it, into a complex system.

INNOVATION IN STRUCTURE, GOVERNANCE, AND FINANCE

Perhaps the most significant and intriguing innovation at SOF is its partnership with Microsoft. Interestingly, however, none of Microsoft's inputs are overtly related to the use of technology in educational innovation, as most lay people would define it. Microsoft did not claim that technology is a panacea; rather, it wanted to explore whether having a corporate partner could bring technical assistance and insight into education. From the school's inception, Microsoft has provided resources in four distinct capacities.

First, it has offered periodic financial support. According to SOF staff, the only financial contribution that Microsoft made was a $100,000 donation that went toward a meeting room in the school. However, another staff member mentioned that Microsoft purchased a tool for keeping a record of teaching performance after running it by the chief learner. Aside from these blips, the extent of Microsoft's financial contributions to the school remains unclear, especially since we have not had access to financial documentation. None of Microsoft's cash contributions, however, have overtly funded technology.

Second, Microsoft provided input on the building design to The Prisco Group architectural firm, which is reflected in the school grounds. The grounds embody the atmosphere of a corporate workspace, such as a food court–style eating area (actually referred to as the food court by learners and staff). Microsoft envisioned a school whose building would provide a sense of small-town community, where one could view the entire school from one end to the other via a "main street." This architecture provides an ideal platform to showcase Microsoft products.

Third, Microsoft gave education-specific input through a contact liaison at company headquarters. Her responsibilities have included provision of new technological teaching tools (e.g., online grading rosters), curriculum aid, and use of the Microsoft Competency Wheel for hiring educators. Microsoft also had input into the initial hiring strategy for educators and the chief learner. Although it appears that most of the input on school curricular choices was in the hands of administration and faculty, the Microsoft contact liaison is a present, positive influence at SOF.

Finally, Microsoft sponsors an on-site liaison who provides technological support and school tours for the public. This worker has a background in sales and is neither a technology nor an education expert. The Microsoft-SOF partnership is not run through Microsoft's Corporate Citizenship office or its community relations department, but through the education-sector sales team. As a member of this team, the on-site liaison has a visible presence throughout the school.

Microsoft's inputs to SOF not only span a range of functions; they also have differing degrees of continuity. The building design is not a continuous function of Microsoft; once the school was built, it was no longer necessary to have design input. The creation of the curriculum is ongoing but not continuous. The contact liaison is useful to the faculty on a case-by-case basis. Financial support seems not to be continuous, and possibly not ongoing. The one-time donations by Microsoft do not appear to be part of a strategic commitment to financial support. The on-site liaison, however, is a continuous function of the partnership.

The Microsoft relationship suggests that there are some fairly significant differences between this partnership and what might be perceived as a "normal" relationship between a company and a school. This is especially true when considering a company-school partnership run out of a corporate foundation or community outreach arm. The primary relationship between SOF and Microsoft does not seem to be financially based, since

Microsoft's funding for this project is not large enough to have a significant impact on how the school operates. Microsoft's main support is also not technology based but administrative. For example, the company helps in personnel crises and provides corporate human resource assistance.

Because the Microsoft-SOF partnership is managed through the sales arm of Microsoft rather than the corporate foundation, there may be significant benefits to the company. One could think of SOF as a giant Microsoft showroom. The benefit of the partnership for Microsoft may be a role in innovative educational reform, but it could also be seen as an innovation in corporate marketing, with some smaller benefits trickling down to the school. SOF was conceived in part as an incubator for new ideas that Microsoft could then disseminate to a wider market.

That said, the relationship between Microsoft and SOF has attracted many additional partners, which certainly benefits the school. As a staff member pointed out, "Our first year . . . everybody under the sun wanted to be a partner with the school . . . So we sort of whittled it down and decided . . . that we would rather have maybe five [partners] and really use them." Having such a range of interested parties has allowed the school to be selective, choosing only partners that will benefit the educational experiences of the student body. None of these partnerships, however, seems necessarily related to technological innovation. SOF's partnerships seem typical of any neighborhood high school. For example, learners receive tutoring from local college students and get exposure to live science through the West Park Cultural and Opportunity Center and the Philadelphia Zoo.

Many financial partners have also donated to the school, but they have not specifically funded educational innovation. For example, Vanguard donated $50,000 for a new technology lab. The lab does benefit the learners, but it is not something new in education. Donors have also funded three staff positions at SOF, including a development coordinator, a guidance counselor, and a systems engineer. These positions are a sign of a larger governance capability, but none constitutes an innovative approach. According to staff members, the school had several major donors at its inception who made "significant contributions," but SOF is "not actively seeking donors." In keeping with district regulations, all funding must go through the central office at the district before it can be distributed to SOF.

Although Microsoft is an essential partner to SOF, the school is nonetheless a public, comprehensive school within the School District of Philadelphia. The district remains an omnipresent force in the school's structure, governance, daily operations, and curriculum. This presence seems evident to faculty and staff, as one educator explained: "We are a regular school. We have the same traditional budget . . . Our principal is a School District of Philadelphia principal who has the . . . same criteria and has the things come down from leadership that have to be done."

This sentiment highlights the lack of financial innovation in the school. Aside from the start-up cost of $60 million appropriated for construction, the way SOF "does business" is not unique in the budgetary eyes of the district. Although no financial documentation was provided to us, school faculty and district officials made it clear that the school operates under the same financial regulations as other public high schools. A part-time district employee who splits her time between three different schools in Philadelphia oversees SOF's financials. She says that SOF operates in exactly the same way as other district schools, although per-pupil spending is possibly slightly higher at SOF because of the costs of operating the new facility.

Applying the district's funding formula, the basic allocation of funding per high school student is $10,907. Revisiting the production-function metaphor, there is some evidence of minor innovative "technology" in terms of how the school is sourcing, allocating, and accounting for resources. For example, the school decided not to purchase textbooks. It is also able to secure some in-kind resources.

In terms of governance, a huge constraint (and perhaps a laudable one to undertake) is that the school has chosen to work within the boundaries set by the district. SOF is not a charter or a private school. Each new SOF chief learner has had to contend with increasing constraints on the curriculum. District constraints have further increased restrictions on educational innovation, due to the importance state performance exams have in funding. In this way, SOF is no different from any other high school in Philadelphia.

District restrictions were especially noticeable in the distinct histories of SOF's chief learners. The first chief learner did not have any experience working in the School District of Philadelphia. The current chief learner, in contrast, has a history as both a leader in Philadelphia's public schools and a manager in the district's central office. In hiring new educators, the current chief learner does not look for anything particularly different than she would have in her other school leadership positions. The shift in leadership is felt among the faculty, one of whom noted that "our new leadership is trying to make it known that we are a Philadelphia public school."

Changes in leadership have altered governance of the faculty. The first chief learner gave educators complete autonomy over the school's curriculum. This fluid approach generated extremely high potential for educational innovation, as each classroom became its own curricular laboratory. Classrooms then were trial-and-error testing areas of educational inputs, analogous to the production function described earlier. Even with the loss of the first chief learner, a sense of curricular autonomy among the faculty seems to have been retained. As one educator explained, "You have very strong personalities in this building, and everybody wants to be the leader. Because when the school opened up, everybody [was] supposed to be the leader." Although there may be some disharmony among the faculty over the appropriate degree of educator autonomy, one thing is clear: SOF continues to promote a working environment that fosters flexibility in curriculum design and organizational structure.

Continual changes in leadership, compounded by district constraints, have led to a reduction in educator autonomy and pressure to conform to district standards. The future of the school's fluid and innovative organizational nature is in question. Some faculty members seem cynical about how their autonomy can survive in a landscape of trying to meet districtwide curriculum and state test requirements. Others are more optimistic. As one educator remarked, "For two years, we were trying to write a curriculum. I'm saying, what's wrong with the district's? It's just how you're going to teach it [that matters]. But you have to know what you have to teach, what's going to be covered." According to some educators, SOF needs to be more grounded instead of attempting curricular innovation.

Another input that warrants discussion is students. There has been a lot of research on the significance of peers in the learning process. SOF characterizes itself as a neighborhood school and uses a lottery system to select its student body. The experiment of SOF was designed to support students in the neighborhood rather than to build an elite cohort. It is perhaps the one "technology" that was intentionally designed to be traditional.

HARDWARE AND SOFTWARE: IS NEW TECHNOLOGY NECESSARILY INNOVATIVE?

Microsoft was explicit in not advocating technology as a panacea in education reform. Indeed, SOF's first design principle was "learning first, technology later." Nevertheless, one has the sense that technology itself is part of the school's vision. This is evidenced by the many new computers in the student center, which also showcases Microsoft's "new" products. Each classroom has Promethean boards (interactive whiteboards) and webcams for educator demonstrations, Dell Tablet computers in math and English classrooms, and voice enhancers, which many educators use to amplify their voices. Each SOF learner has a laptop and the school has wireless Internet access—albeit with somewhat spotty coverage. The school uses Microsoft and Microsoft-affiliated software systems and uses a portal to connect learners, educators, and families via an online site.

The school's learning center houses a tabletop computer called a Microsoft Surface, which functions much like a handheld touchpad, but in large, horizontal form. While the Microsoft Surface may eventually be available for everyone at SOF, the on-site liaison has made it clear that this tool serves primarily as a tester model to find out how educators might experiment with it in the classroom. In essence, SOF has not yet determined any substantive educational function for Microsoft Surface, and it therefore serves as a poignant symbol for our analysis of hardware and software. As it currently stands, the use of technology to facilitate both administration and learning at SOF seems limited. Many tools are in place, but the system has not adopted them.

Operational Challenges

At an operational level, there have been several stumbling blocks presented by SOF's technologies. Although the school promotes itself as a wireless environment, many educators and students complain that Internet access is spotty. One educator even complained that "the wireless network is horrible." Other educators and students expressed problems with the usability of the online portal, noting that many do not know how to employ it correctly.

Learner laptop use also presents a major challenge, since many learners have never had access to them before. As one educator explained, "A lot of them had never had a computer or laptop and were doing the MySpace thing and Skype and things that are like, okay, but I need you to bring it back. And they're fourteen; they were more excited that their computer had these functions." During class, learners engage in activities like shopping online, playing games, chatting with friends, and visiting gossip sites such as MySpace and Facebook. We witnessed many learners surfing the Internet, sometimes right in front of their educators' eyes.

Currently, SOF is investing in a new laptop-monitoring program, which will allow educators to check on learners' Internet activity and curb distractions. One educator suggested that some students might need to have their laptops taken away and "revert to paper and pencil" because they are not responsible enough. Laptops can also create contemporary excuses for not turning in work, such as, "My e-mail didn't send right" or "The computer deleted my file."

SOF has also addressed compatibility issues, especially as it tries to align itself with the rest of the district, which largely uses Apple technologies. There are no district systems in place to support Microsoft-centered technologies. As SOF tries to integrate with the district, it faces technological challenges when systems and software are incompatible.

Theory Versus Practice

As mentioned above, SOF provides a laptop for each student in the school. The laptops are the property of the district and are on loan to SOF. Educators, learners, and administrators told us that many students were receiving their first laptop ever, which was a source of excitement, delight, and honor. Some students told us that at first they did not believe they would be allowed to keep their laptops for an entire four years. Students use their laptops both inside and outside school. Ideally, this enables them to make a fluid transition from classwork to homework.

Initially, many students were unfamiliar with the fragility of laptops, but most of the students seem to treat them with respect. We heard a few stories of students throwing or slamming down their laptops, which caused the district to purchase heavier, more durable units. When students forget to bring their laptops to school, they typically have to write by hand during class.

Although laptops are in use at SOF, their contribution to improvements in learning remain dubious, due to obstacles at the organizational level. For instance, while SOF staff told us that many students do not have much facility with technology, no actions have been taken to remedy this. One educator said, "We're losing a lot of the kids with the technology because they're not used to it. They were given computers and they weren't given computer classes." Another educator noted that students arrived with "almost zero technological skills. They didn't know how to type . . . the extent of their competencies was finding a Web page, finding IM." SOF's emphasis on integrating technology into the curriculum is laudable, but some initial training for educators and learners would be helpful.

Because SOF does not have a separate technology curriculum, there is only a disaggregated model for how educators determine students' level of technology proficiency. This kind of educator autonomy and adaptability might make sense if educators had a lot of experience with technology, but most do not. As one educator said, "I am a terrible technology teacher because I had to struggle on my own to use it. So between me not explaining it the best [way] and them not knowing how to use it, it was a perfect storm." Gradually, the Microsoft on-site liaison and other SOF staff members who are adept with technology have begun to offer assistance and suggestions, and they are developing adaptive, customized classroom support. To date, however, SOF has not been able to leverage these tools in the way that was originally envisioned.

SOF's shifts in leadership have also influenced the use of these tools. During the first year, educators engaged students in individual and collaborative "project-based" learning and promoted activities like "webquests" and blogs. SOF technologies also enabled administrative flexibility. Learners and educators had rapidly changing daily schedules, a practice that was tied to the adaptability the first administration wanted to promote. Aided by the online portal, new schedules could easily be uploaded, e-mailed, and available in real time. An SOF staff member noted the following regarding the research and development at the school:

> One of their tenets, one of the things they say you have to believe, is that you can fail and you can make mistakes. This process is very messy, and we would design these schedules for kids who had never had this kind of experience before . . . You'd put a schedule in place and it would be the absolute most bad decision you could have made.

Other educators echo these sentiments about how technological systems and flexibility fueled the workings of the school during that first year. There is a sense of nostalgia among administrators and educators who enjoyed the sense of camaraderie and creativity in the open environment. There is also a sense of resentment among newer educators and administrators who wish they had been at the school during that time. Only a few educators, veterans of other Philadelphia public schools, seem to think SOF's process of utilizing technology has been too open for high school learners.

The present use of technology at SOF is more constrained, due to shifts in administrative and curricular goals. Learners do less project-based learning and more within a standards-driven curriculum. They use laptops mainly to complete assignments, much as any high school student might. The use of laptops at SOF does not seem to be linked to any particularly useful innovation. We have no way of knowing how students might be using their laptops and engaging in project-based learning if SOF were not currently concentrating on aligning itself more closely with the district's curriculum. SOF still plans to return eventually to a more innovative, project-based vision.

In addition to district requirements to teach the standards-based curriculum, individual teaching styles also have affected the amount and type of technological use. In one math class, an educator uses the Promethean board much like a chalkboard, while learners write their notes on a paper worksheet (with their laptops closed and unused). From this observation, it is questionable how different the Promethean board is from a standard dry-erase board—the process of completing the problem did not necessarily seem more effective. However, this educator also uses a webcam to demonstrate calculator functions on the Promethean board so that learners can observe what she was doing.

In a language arts and history class, learners use the Promethean board to showcase PowerPoint, a rather common tool in classrooms. Both this class and the math class suggest that technology has mainly upgraded the traditional techniques of education, rather than fundamentally changing the educational model. Moreover, some educators have resisted using technology altogether in the classroom, preferring more traditional methods of instruction. As one educator asserted, "All I need [is] chalk and an eraser and I'm good to go . . . Everything cannot be on a computer . . . The school was built and they didn't put any funding in for projects. So how are you going to have a science lab if you don't have anything [for] science? Everything should not be virtual. You've got to hold a frog."

In this instance, the educator thought that an overemphasis on technological equipment was not providing enough hands-on experiences for learners. Another educator told us, "When they are with me, we don't use laptops . . . they need to have times where they do things hands on." Schools, of course, need to make difficult decisions about the kinds of equipment and resources they want to invest in, and what kinds of exposure and educational experiences they want learners to have. Although SOF does not provide much in the way of science equipment or printed materials, it does equip learners with laptops, which they cherish. While eating lunch in SOF's food court, one student told us that he shares his laptop with his siblings at home, taking turns in the evening and allowing family members to benefit from SOF's resources.

While there may well be examples of innovative use, SOF has not fully leveraged the application of learning tools in the classroom. New technologies may afford new ways of thinking, creating, connecting, and collaborating, thus allowing students to direct their own learning, have more agency, and be more engaged in their education. However, if educators use new technologies in old ways (such as using a Promethean board much as one would use a chalkboard), then technological possibilities may be unduly limited. The current variability in use and application—combined with having more regulation from the district—may have stalled the ubiquitous adoption of these tools to enhance learning in innovative ways.

INNOVATIONS IN CURRICULUM?

First-Year Curriculum

During year one, SOF administrators and staff worked collaboratively to develop their own project-based curriculum. As one staff member described, "When we started in 2006, it was just thirteen of us at a table . . . We worked really, really hard. And we had to put this place together from scratch." First-year SOF educators and administrators show excitement and pride in their curriculum-development efforts. They worked hard to bring their theories about ideal learning into practice, had many opportunities to be creative, and felt a sense of empowerment. Another staff member said, "In that first year . . . we were really designing. We'd say, 'What do we want the schedule to look like? Oh, what if we can do this? Let's see, can we? Let's call these people, let's see.' So the approach was very teamwork [oriented] and 'what if' and optimistic."

As educators engaged in project-based learning at SOF, they found that learners responded positively to opportunities that enabled them to guide their own learning. One educator said, "We saw so much in that first year of qualitative evidence of things working . . . We were seeing this group that should statistically become disengaged and drop out, and they're coming to school every day . . . They're engaged, they're working on these projects." Students also attested to positive learning experiences that first year. As one learner told us,

> It was fun. We had a lot of great projects. That's the year we had the best proj-
> ects. I remember for a long period of time we were working on a UN, United
> Nations project. Everybody used to come here from all over the world and
> we'd just learn about different people. We were learning our new programs,
> just getting familiar with the school, finding our place.

A key element to the curriculum during the first year was project-based learning. Projects enabled educator creativity, learner-directed learning, an innovative assessment system (without numerical or letter grades), and trial and error. For example, SOF's assessment system included the following categories: advanced, proficient, basic, novice, and "not on the radar" (did not complete the assignment). Rather than a traditional letter grade, learners were given lengthy feedback on assignments. Without grades, however, there was no indication of how student assessments stacked up cumulatively or with respect to their peers. As one student said, "It was a little bit confusing because when you got your report card . . . it was, like, so many pages. It had every assignment from every class, and then it had proficient, novice. It was hard to understand because, okay, I got a novice on this assignment, I got a proficient on this assignment, I got a basic on this. So what do I have overall?" Providing lengthy feedback to learners is certainly admirable, but they also seemed to be acutely interested in knowing their overall standing.

First-year staff conveyed a sense of nostalgia over the freedom they had had to shape curricular developments. Nonetheless, the opportunity to create a curriculum from the ground up had left some educators (especially newer ones) feeling unprepared for their classes. One educator, for example, had been trained in English but found himself teaching many other courses. He explained, "When I got here I was thrown a roster. I was teaching six different preps. I had violin lessons, I had drama classes, theater classes, movies, a class in cinema, script writing, American history. I taught some math skills and I taught English." Another educator said that on most mornings, he would show up at the school and not know who or what he would be teaching that day. Instead, he would receive an e-mail that detailed his teaching load.

The uncertainty of the schedule and open-ended curriculum also affected learners. One learner told us that in the first year they "got a different schedule [e-mailed] every day." The school's open system was exciting but perhaps not initially appropriate for SOF learners. Not only were most of them unfamiliar with the use of technology, but they also were behind academically. As one educator noted, over 60 percent of SOF students arrived at the school behind in reading, writing, and math: "We can't do this pie in the sky abstract thing because they [learners] are missing pieces."

Second and Third Years

In the summer of SOF's second year, many of the educators banded together to develop a new curriculum. With a different chief learner and greater district oversight, however, the flexible curriculum option was tabled in favor of the district core curriculum. The central office was also concerned about SOF learners being able to transfer between schools. As one staff member explained, "The idea was that we weren't transparent or transferable . . . and if any child wanted to leave for any reason, they couldn't because it didn't work with any other school in the district." Furthermore, the district and some in the SOF community thought the school's experimental curriculum was unfair to students.

While some educators resent this shift away from autonomy of educator-developed curriculum, others have recognized the flaws of such a flexible, untested curriculum. As one current staff member explained, "That's one of the lessons learned. If I had this to do all over again, we would not open our front doors until . . . [the curriculum] was all fleshed out, with everything worked out." After the first year, SOF was strongly encouraged to implement more traditional methods of teaching. For instance, SOF now uses letter grades to assess learners and concentrates on aligning itself with district mandates. Overall, SOF seems to have begun at one extreme of flexibility and autonomy and now to be swinging toward a much more rigid, preplanned curriculum.

In the third year since the opening of SOF, the school has struggled to develop a curriculum that intertwines its philosophy—an emphasis on technology governing a socially mediated curricular approach—with district standards. While the leadership has remained hopeful, many staff have felt strained by having to adjust so much in the last three years. As one educator said, "They [some educators] have never taught the core curriculum and now we're grappling—Where are we going to start? In the beginning of the curriculum? In the middle of the curriculum? Where are they going to start?—and they [school administrators] can't answer you."

Another educator spoke of the emotional toll and frustration of concentrating on district standards instead of particular learner needs: "The systems and the bureaucracy, they just kind of wear you down in a district like this, knowing that you need to do something for a kid, but knowing that it takes levels and obstacles and hurdles to get that service, or that person, or this agency, or whatever it might be." Emphasis on district standards, after having envisioned a school with an open curricular system, has brought disorganization and confusion. Changes in curricular goals have also created tension among educators, some of whom miss the old days and some of whom welcome the district's increased oversight. More dialogue among SOF educators would help both groups learn from each others' perspectives and strengths.

SOF still has a somewhat rapidly changing schedule throughout the school year. Students are on a three-month cycle, with new educators and classes every three months. One educator complained about the lack of continuity: "Every three months you're getting a new group of kids." These adjustments may be difficult for both educators and learners. Another SOF educator noted that "these kids have not had a single, solid year of any subject at all . . . Like for American history, I had one group . . . then in November, I got a whole new group of kids. Then the same thing happened again." This rapid rotation may be too much for some educators, especially those who are used to a more traditional academic schedule. SOF's continued emphasis on adaptability in the midst of reconciling its adherence to district standards is important and may ultimately lead back to its original vision. In the short term, though, it may add stress to the environment.

SOF's curriculum now blends self-directed learning, technological innovations, transparency in student assessments (ensuring that grades are compatible with college applications), and standard core curricular subjects. The school also seems to attract students to preprofessional, business/technology career options, perhaps due to Microsoft's presence. Many students we talked to had professional goals—to go into business or information technology or to work specifically for Microsoft. One student told us, "This school, to me, is a business preparatory school and that's what I want to pursue in my career." SOF is also launching an IT support certification program, in which students will be trained and certified in information technology.

THE SCHOOL OF *THE* FUTURE? OR, *A* SCHOOL OF *A* FUTURE?

In various stages of development, SOF has focused on creating an adaptable school environment, equipping students with technological access, and engaging them in project-based learning. It has had to attempt these innovations within the constraints posed by the School District of Philadelphia. As a consequence, SOF is currently trying to focus on the district's standards-based curriculum as a primary goal. At this point, SOF seems to be a standards-focused comprehensive high school, spiced up with high-tech equipment.

Given that the school is called School of the Future, an important question to consider is, *what* future does the school envision for its students after graduation? Our data indicate that SOF is preparing students for both college and career opportunities, especially those that are IT or business oriented. SOF's mission states that the school aims to "prepare our students for the future workforce or optimize their entry into a college, university, or technical school of their choice." Although this dual direction is embedded in the school's mission, whether SOF can fulfill its mission remains to be seen; its first class will graduate in 2010.

Some educators and learners argue that SOF's experimental projects and assessments may have jeopardized students' college applications. One educator stated, "The students are very frustrated. They are very concerned about their grades . . . about getting into college." One student informed us that applying to college is "one of the criteria for even graduating." We also received evidence, however, that some students were not considering college. One educator said that he polled his class to see how many of them planned to attend college, and only one of thirty raised his hand. It is interesting that, given the demographics of the students (and that it is not a magnet school), there was a debate occurring around the school's focus. It is unclear whether SOF will meet its goal of seeing many of its students matriculate at college, but it does have them talking about postsecondary opportunities. This is a step in the right direction.

Science Leadership Academy

We examined four other high schools as a benchmark to compare our conclusions about SOF. Science Leadership Academy (SLA) is a public magnet high school formed through a partnership between the School District of Philadelphia and the Franklin Institute. It operates within many of the same constraints as SOF, although a significant difference is that it can select its students. Its partnership with the Franklin Institute also affords extra educational opportunities to students, such as museum visits.

SLA encourages students to define their own learning through projects, which are assessed with a rubric that is transferable across the district. Teachers act as curriculum designers and are all involved in decision making. SLA offers state-of-the-art technology, including laptops for students. Like SOF, it does not focus explicitly on technology, believing that technology should be an "invisible" learning tool. SLA does offer technological instruction for its students.

In looking at what its students do after graduation, SLA is undoubtedly college preparatory. Over 90 percent of its current students are headed to a four-year college or university. While SLA seems on the surface to share many of the same attributes and values as SOF, but with more successful outcomes, the one obvious difference is that SLA is a special-admit school that hand selects its students, whereas SOF accepts anyone who is chosen via lottery.

Penn Charter

William Penn Charter School is Philadelphia's oldest independent private school. Penn Charter selects students through an application process. It offers high-tech equipment, including Promethean boards in most classrooms, wireless Internet access, and laptops for in-school use. Like SOF, Penn Charter initially experienced problems with spotty wireless Internet access, but it has since increased its bandwidth.

Penn Charter says that it does not want to be so cutting edge that its technology, curriculum, or pedagogy is experimental, but it does want to keep up with technological trends. The school offers some autonomy to teachers in terms of curricular design but provides administrative support as well. Penn Charter is also a college preparatory school, and nearly 100 percent of its students attend college.

As a private school, there are clearly limitations to what Penn Charter can offer compared to a public school like SOF. However, we found Penn Charter's technologies to be remarkably similar to SOF's in terms of providing laptops, Internet access, Promethean boards, etc. SOF does not seem to offer anything technologically that cannot be found in other schools.

Pennsylvania Virtual High School and K12 Inc.

K12 Inc. is a corporation that manages public schools throughout the country, reaching over 55,000 students. It is an entirely online group of schools that incorporate a student-focused, individualized curriculum. Students also learn offline, as K12 sends materials to students' homes, where students engage in activities and homework assignments under the guidance of their parents.

This corporation-school partnership attempts to use a technological medium to provide student-directed learning. K12 also expects a high degree of parental involvement in guiding learning, and in that sense, students and families are self-selected. Students who participate in K12 learn within their own homes, which in many cases requires a stay-at-home parent or child-care arrangement.

K12 seeks to teach communications skills, reading skills, analytic skills, and more. It says that with the advent of new technologies, it is merely the technological tools that are changing, not the focus on student learning. However, because K12 does rely on technology, it trains teachers to use its systems.

LITMUS TEST: INPUTS AND OUTPUTS

To provide a litmus test for school innovation, we have created table 3.1, which ranks the schools according to the quality of various inputs and outputs. In facing all the challenges of our most under-resourced schools and without much evidence of technological innovation in the most broadly construed sense, we see that SOF has yet to realize its vision.

CREATING AND SUSTAINING INNOVATION

SOF is a unique public-private partnership with an innovative vision, an evolving curriculum, and a number of ongoing challenges. The school offers both positive attributes and unrealized potential. SOF certainly provides its students with remarkable facilities and technological equipment. Attending such a new, beautiful, and well-cared-for school can have a positive effect on student experiences. One educator relayed the following story:

> I was talking to a kid. We were talking about—the kid has a twin. He was talking about how his twin's misbehaving, beating on the walls. I said, "Why don't you behave like your twin?" He says, "Because I'm here." I said, "What do you mean by that?" He said, "Well, if I were [at] some trashy old school, I'd be doing the same thing. It's the building that makes me behave." So, I feel . . . simply being in a building filled with light, there's no bars on the windows, it's beautiful, it's open, it's spacious. The mind set it gives the kids, even if we screw everything else up, to walk into a building like this puts you in a space of, I'm here to do something different. I'm here to do something special.

TABLE 3.1
Technological innovation in schools

School	Student selection	Governance	Finances	Curriculum	Technology	Partnership	Student success
School of the Future	4 (lottery)	4 (regular school, reports to regional head)	2 (PPE plus)	4 (district core curriculum)	3 laptops, wireless, Promethean boards, new products (Microsoft)	3 (Microsoft)	4 (38.7 math and 47.3 reading in Pennsylvania System of School Assessment [PSSA])
William Penn Charter School	1 (highly selective)	1 (private school)	1 ($24,000 per student)	1 (independent college prep)	2 Promethean boards, TI calculators, students sign out laptops and iPods (Apple)	4 (Friends Council)	1 (middle 50 percent SAT reasoning test 1760–2100)
Science Leadership Academy	2 (magnet)	3 (reports to special district superintendent)	2 (PPE plus)	2 (aligned with core but project-based)	4 laptops (Apple)	1 (Franklin Institute)	2 (75.1 math and 83.6 reading in PSSA)
Pennsylvania Virtual High School	3 (self-selective)	2 (autonomous, reports to state)	4 (less than PPE)	3 (autonomous, meets state standards)	1 entirely online	2 (K12)	3 (60 math and 66.7 reading in PSSA)

Note: Per pupil expenditure (PPE) for Philadelphia is $10,907, and the proportion of students proficient or above on the state assessment is 37.4 percent in reading and 32.6 percent in math for eleventh graders in 2008. Numbers 1–4 indicate our ranking of each school's degree of challenge in inputs and outputs, with 4 as the highest.

SOF students do seem to feel valued by their school and are concerned about the direction it will take. SOF is still challenged in manifesting its vision, given its goals of operating as a comprehensive high school within the constraints of an urban district.

One of the inherent difficulties of being a research-and-development school like SOF is that the future prospects of students are at stake while the school is experimenting with educational resources. As one educator said, "The problem is, you can't keep switching and trying things when you're dealing with the lives of children." In the midst of all these changes and tensions, educational experiences are altered. Among the excitement and frustrations during the first few years of SOF's operations, there are several lessons to be learned.

The first lesson is a financial one. SOF operates under regular district constraints, but it has also benefited from donations. SOF's unique partnership with Microsoft clearly helped leverage some of the start-up costs. Affordances like a new building and technological equipment seem to enhance students' experiences and, subsequently, their sense of pride and self-worth. While the constraint of operating the budget within standard district guidelines suggests the potential for scalability, the start-up costs to build the new facility are discouraging for realizing scale.

There was no fundamental innovation in the allocation of resources at SOF that would allow for significant improvement in costs and benefits. The lesson is that the emphasis needs to be on finding new and creative ways to allocate resources. SOF and other innovators within the district systems should focus their energies in this area. Another option is to expand dramatically the growth of charter schools, which are not constrained in the same ways as SOF. It is worthwhile for a school to consider how it can creatively direct money when operating within a district and complying with financing rules.

These financing constraints also demonstrate a lesson about curriculum. SOF's curricular tensions illustrate the difficulty of maintaining an innovative vision while operating under greater academic rules, such as a standardized core curriculum. This does not mean that educational innovation must exist outside a public school system. Rather, innovative schools must ensure that their assessment systems and curricular models are transferable across schools and districts. In hindsight, the laudable vision that launched this endeavor could have benefited from being tempered with more explicit district constraints. That way, the curriculum model would be transparent not only to the district but also to colleges and future employers.

This latter point offers a third lesson. In addition to innovating within curricular constraints, the SOF model highlights the importance of determining whether a school is college preparatory, career preparatory, or both, and subsequently ensuring that the curriculum is developed accordingly. In doing so, schools must communicate their mission to parents, families, and students so that students can choose the type of school that best meets their needs and goals.

Finally, innovative schools must consider how they want to integrate technology into the curriculum and train educators and students appropriately. Schools need to assess what kinds of abilities educators and students already have and delineate areas where support is needed. Much of this may need to be customized according to the ability of the school's population. In the case of SOF, formalizing technology coursework as part of the curriculum could have benefited faculty and students, in addition to integrating technology into the curriculum.

Despite all the changes over the past few years, SOF has still managed to create a school community in which students feel valued by, and value, their school. SOF learners have a real affection for the school. As one third-year learner told us, "I'm still proud to be here. That's not going to change anything because we are the first class, and even though there were a lot of changes, we still grew from it." Another learner said of SOF, "Everything I learned here is relevant to my future. I love it. I love the school." If SOF can continue to engage students and realize its educational vision of innovation, it may indeed become an important model for public education.

SOF represents a comprehensive public high school's potential to offer enriching, innovative educational experiences and to equip students with technological tools that they will use. Many of SOF's ongoing challenges result from attempting to create an innovative, flexible, comprehensive high school that gives a high degree of autonomy to educators, all within the confines of the district. We cannot yet say how SOF's curriculum will develop, how it will integrate technology into the classroom over the long term, or what kind of postsecondary outcomes will be realized: that is a chapter for the future. The key is to understand that a crucial component of innovation is to balance it with the impact that learning has on the community. This is critical to ensuring that there is sufficient stability to create a truly innovative school.

4

The Challenge of Sustainable Leadership

Matthew Riggan and Margaret E. Goertz

THE STORY OF School of the Future is in no small measure a story of leadership. It is a story that unfolds at every level of the school system, from the CEO's office to the classroom. It offers lessons about why committed leadership is essential to sustaining innovation and why such leadership is itself so difficult to sustain. It highlights the essential role of school and district leaders in creating organizational conditions for instructional innovation. Above all, it speaks to the centrality of leaders in negotiating the complex relationship between local innovation and systemwide norms, compliance and risk, ambiguity and familiarity. Although its founding partner is Microsoft, the story of leadership at SOF is not really a story about technology. By design, technology served the school's vision, but it did not drive it. What made the school innovative was a radically different approach to curriculum, instruction, assessment, and school organization. Far more than technology, it was these characteristics that defined leadership at SOF.

WHY LEADERSHIP MATTERS

Despite widespread agreement that leadership is vital to the success of districts, schools, and, ultimately, students, the relationship between leadership and student learning is complex and indirect. Attempts to analyze the impact principals have on student achievement, for example, have shown modest effects at best. There is more evidence that school leaders are instrumental in creating organizational conditions under which high-quality teaching and learning can occur.[1] More conclusive still is the literature on the role of school leadership in implementing reforms. A litany of policy studies and program evaluations highlights the role of leadership in facilitating and sustaining organizational change. Equally important, it is nearly impossible to find cases where school- or district-level reforms were successfully implemented in the absence of committed, capable leadership.[2]

School change cannot happen without strong leadership from principals and superintendents. But the commitment and capability of the top of the organizational hierarchy is frequently insufficient to facilitate real, sustainable change in classrooms. In the last decade, a broader, distributed view of leadership has become increasingly common. In this view, leadership is understood as a form of work through which the attitudes, knowledge, or behaviors of people in schools are influenced. This work, which may be undertaken by anyone in a school or by groups of people irrespective of their position, is often done collaboratively.[3]

ENVISIONING LEADERSHIP

In designing SOF, Microsoft and the School District of Philadelphia did not prescribe a specific leadership model. Instead, they sought to create the basic conditions under which the work of leadership would be carried out. These conditions were shaped by two major elements: first, the centrality of professional leadership, and second, the development of a set of education competencies, which, among other things, guided the hiring process for both the chief learner and educators.

Professional Leadership

SOF design documents identified professional leadership as one of five factors schools need to meet the demands of a twenty-first-century, global society successfully. Explained as a form of human capital, professional leadership included:

> The ability to (1) impact instruction positively; (2) think strategically; (3) motivate and engage stakeholders; (4) engage technology at every appropriate opportunity; (5) design and present professional development to address identified needs; (6) interact and communicate with the community; (7) demonstrate fiscal responsibility; and (8) continuously evaluate and revise the instructional program in a collaborative manner. The ultimate professional leader understands the necessity to serve and subconsciously walks and talks the vision, mission, and belief statements.[4]

With the exception of emphasizing the use of technology, these abilities are fairly consistent with research about what effective school leadership requires.[5] But the role of leadership at SOF differed from these perspectives in two important respects. First, professional leadership did not exclusively refer to the abilities of the chief learner; it was a quality sought in all staff members. Second, organizational fixtures in traditional school settings—grade levels, marking periods, fixed schedules or subject areas—were not assumed at SOF. The role of leadership was to create, through both design and daily practice, an organization that reflected and supported the school's vision. This would prove to be one of the most radical, innovative, and challenging aspects of the SOF design.

Education Competencies

To identify and recruit a chief learner with the desired abilities, Microsoft and the Philadelphia school district worked with a leadership-development firm to create a set of education competencies that were intended to "describe the full range of characteristics to help a school district achieve its organizational goals and vision."[6] As this language suggests, the goal in developing these competencies extended beyond SOF. Like many aspects of the design process, they were created as a resource for other schools and districts seeking to launch similar efforts. The result of this work was an education competency wheel (figure 4.1) divided into six areas: individual

FIGURE 4.1
Education competency wheel

Source: Reprinted with permission from the Microsoft Corporation.

excellence; organizational skills; courage; results; strategic skills; and operating skills.[7]

The education competencies were intended to guide SOF operations in everything from the assessment of student work to professional development,
and they heavily influenced the hiring process. In part due to Microsoft's
own approach to talent management and in part due to the fact that SOF was

brand new, the school's design relied heavily—indeed, almost exclusively—on getting the right people in place. This is both logical and markedly different from the way that most school systems (limited as they are in terms of whom they recruit and how they hire) approach talent management.

Both the articulation of professional leadership and the education competencies suggest the need for particular leadership skills. The prominence of collaboration both within and beyond the school demanded a leader who could effectively solicit and incorporate feedback from multiple sources and constituencies, build relationships, and devolve authority and decision making. Similarly, the emphasis on flexibility and adaptability—most directly embodied in the goal of creating a "continuous, relevant, and adaptive" learning environment—suggested that while guided by a clear, consistent vision, school leaders needed to be able to continually revisit and renew their assumptions about daily school practice.[8] This called for a dynamic understanding of how that vision might be carried out, the skills to quickly reorganize and redeploy resources (e.g., funding, staff, and instructional time) to support adaptation, and the ability to systematically monitor and evaluate progress.

FROM VISION TO ACTION

The SOF design placed enormous responsibility on the school's chief learner. The hiring process, designed by Microsoft in partnership with the School District of Philadelphia, was detailed and rigorous. It began by soliciting applications electronically over a short period of time, in part to screen for technological savvy and decisiveness. Thirty days later, the pool of applicants was reduced to seven, who were subsequently interviewed by a community panel. Three finalists for the position were identified during this round of interviews. These finalists participated in a final round of seven interviews, known as the Loop, in which each interview asked different types of questions and focused on different competencies. Each interviewer rendered a decision to hire or not, based on the candidates' performance in their specific domains.[9]

On September 1, 2005, the first chief learner was hired, a full year before
the school was scheduled to open. She enjoyed the unqualified support of
the district and was given considerable latitude in guiding the school from
vision to reality. She was permitted to hire her own staff and was not required to adhere to the district's core curriculum, a requirement for comprehensive high schools. And while the school would eventually be held
accountable for student performance, the administration of the Pennsylvania System of School Assessment (PSSA) for secondary schools occurred
only in eleventh grade. Because SOF opened with only ninth graders and
was scheduled to add one cohort per year, the PSSA administration would
not occur until the end of the school's third year.

In hiring a faculty, the chief learner employed the same Loop interview
process through which she was hired. In the late spring of 2006, thirteen
educators were hired for the school's first year of operation. While a few
had extensive experience, the majority were either brand new to teaching
or in their first few years in the classroom.

The timing of faculty hiring necessitated a certain amount of on-the-fly
development. The inaugural year at SOF was spent inventing and reinventing the school, sometimes on a daily basis. The school's master schedule
provided an outline for how time would be managed, but it was continu-
ously revised and adapted in response to emergent problems, questions,
or themes within the projects. An educator described the chief learner's
approach: "The chief learner really believed you could . . . create a culture
of absolute fluid motion and movement, and do what you need to do when
you need to do it. And your needs are always changing, so your schedule's
always changing. She really firmly believed that you can do that."

While indicating that part of this fluidity was simply a matter of necessity, the chief learner suggested that the overarching purpose was to ensure
that the interaction of educators and learners guided all other decisions:

> We were committed to keeping it fluid, committed to making sure that . . .
> form supported function. And so, that meant, "Okay, then, let's see: If you
> could figure out that tomorrow you'd like to take half the kids and you want

to be at the zoo half the day, then let me fix that schedule so that you could have what you needed to make sure to make it happen," so that the schedule didn't bind them and the curriculum didn't bind them.

The organization of work was highly collaborative. Educators assumed key administrative responsibilities, such as discipline and scheduling, while the chief learner often worked directly with learners. There was little visible evidence of an organizational hierarchy. Roles and tasks were taken on— some long term, others in passing—as needs emerged. As the chief learner explained, this was driven by both practical necessity and the leadership philosophy:

> I think that when we get locked into a position's description . . . we don't tend to grow, and perhaps don't even get to use other talents that we have, because this is the role we're supposed to do. You only teach in the classroom or you only answer the telephone or . . . whatever the roles are . . . And I think it's a place where you better each individual and then, as each individual plays out growing, then they better the organization.

The leadership work carried out by the chief learner and the faculty during the school's first year reflected SOF's core design principles. Learning for both staff and students was continuous and adaptive, and reflected in the constant revision of learning plans and instructional activities. Through it all, the abiding focus was on the need to learn with and from students. A familiar refrain from the chief learner was that students were vital contributors to the school as a learning community. As a result, the instructional work at SOF needed to honor, challenge, and build on their knowledge.

While the process of inventing a school was exhilarating, it was also draining and at times chaotic. The core elements of traditional schools—rules, schedules, curriculum, and assessment—were being developed on the fly. Some learners struggled with the lack of structure and reliance on technology. Some district administrators were concerned that the climate of the school was deteriorating, although educators at SOF strongly objected to this accusation. Baseline measures of behavior and discipline at SOF, such as suspensions and serious incidents, were comparable to those of other schools.[10] While this might be expected, given that SOF enrolled many of the same students who attended neighborhood comprehensive high schools, the school was being touted internationally as a new model for educating students, regardless of background. The bar was unquestionably set higher.

A lack of communication between the school and district exacerbated the different perceptions of SOF during its first year. While faculty accumulated qualitative evidence of learners' progress, there were no general measures of learning that the school could present to outsiders. SOF was two years away from PSSA testing, and the chief learner had opted not to administer the district's interim assessments, or benchmarks, as they were aligned with a core curriculum that the school did not follow. The school did not use traditional grades, and the chief learner appeared to make little attempt to translate the work done at SOF into district terms, preferring to focus on matters inside the school. Coupled with concerns about the school climate, this lack of clarity about academic performance created tension between those inside the school and those outside it.

As long as SOF enjoyed the strong support of CEO Paul Vallas, however, these tensions were of relatively little consequence. But in April 2007, just eight months after the school opened, Vallas announced his resignation. Soon after, the chief academic officer, another advocate for the school, also left the district. The rapid transition left SOF without its most influential local supporters.

In May 2007, the chief learner hired a second cohort of ten new educators to accommodate the additional 170 learners projected to enroll at SOF in the fall. Many were completely new to the profession. They were attracted by the school's vision and mission, but like the first cohort, they were also drawn by the chief learner herself. This made it all the more shocking when, in July 2007, she resigned for personal reasons.

The faculty was caught off guard by her departure. As the district searched for an interim replacement, the educators scrambled to plan for the coming year with new staff and no chief learner. The district's assistant superintendent for secondary curriculum and instruction, a former high school principal who had worked on the development of SOF, served as a liaison during the transition period.

In the absence of a formal leader, the educators at SOF took it upon themselves to plan for the next year. Prior to her resignation, the chief learner had decided to organize the educators into teams of three who would work with a fixed group of learners throughout the year, a change from the more fluid approach the year before. With support from Microsoft's liaison, the educators coordinated a series of August planning sessions, which included newly hired educators. They discussed the possibility of adopting a shared leadership model in which the faculty ran the school by committee—an idea ultimately rejected by the district. They also decided to adopt some version of a curriculum—a series of projects sequenced one after another. Finally, they discussed developing an instructional model that could be more easily explained to people outside the school.

While many of these decisions were made to compensate for the absence of a chief learner, they also were made in response to pressure from the district. In July 2007, one of the educators and the Microsoft liaison were asked to present to district leaders a summary of the school's progress to date. In response to mounting concerns, the presentation emphasized the school's record on climate, behavior, maintenance of technology, and qualitative evidence of student learning.

In August 2007, the entire faculty convened for orientation and professional development. The intent was to help the newly hired educators prepare for their incoming learners and to introduce them to the new structure. Morale was a challenge. The newly hired educators ranged from angry to sad to anxious about the chief learner's departure. In her absence, they were unsure of where to turn for help:

> We came in for training and the cohort for that first year of educators . . . they were like, "This is what we do here." But nobody could tell us what Tuesday at 11 a.m. looks like. But they could tell us, "This is what a final project that we did last year looked like." But there was no sense of what happened to create that final project in our training.

The second year at SOF was a tumultuous one. The school's interim chief learner voiced support for the work undertaken by the educators over the summer and did not attempt to influence the planning process. For the educators who had invested time in planning for the year and supporting the new educators, his willingness to defer to their judgment was empowering. For the new educators, however, the absence of a leader with whom they could work closely meant less support than they had anticipated.

For the first three months of the school year, the faculty essentially ran the school. Educator teams were charged with developing their own approaches and strategies in instruction, assessment, and discipline. One team invested significant time in creating a project model that outlined criteria for progressing through projects based on performance. For some of the educators, the freedom and responsibility of inventing new instructional approaches was profoundly rewarding: "It was new, it was different. It was creative. And it was something that I was starting to see in progressive schools through my research. It was like, 'We're on the right track. We don't have a leader, we don't have support, but we're on the right track.'"

Other teams adhered to more traditional instructional approaches and focused more heavily on maintaining discipline. Some educators suggested that a stronger hand was needed to establish greater consensus and more common practices throughout the school.

In November 2007, the interim chief learner left to become principal at another school. His replacement brought an approach wholly different from predecessors. Whereas the first chief learner sought to empower teachers to continually invent the school and the second deferred to their prior work experience, the third restored a more conventional teacher-principal relationship based on clearly defined roles. She also placed greater attention on PSSA preparation and advocated a restoration of grade levels. Many of the educators, accustomed to considerable autonomy and heavily invested in alternative approaches to curriculum, instruction, and assessment, resisted these efforts. Morale suffered among both first- and second-year educators.

The school became more fragmented. Several faculty members sensed that SOF was drifting from its vision. The first chief learner, a steward of that vision, was gone. Teams worked in relative isolation, developing their own instructional approaches, assessments, and discipline systems. First- and second-year educators were physically separated from one another and had little formal opportunity to collaborate. Despite an increased focus on traditional discipline over the course of the year, rules and consequences varied across teams and were inconsistently enforced. Many educators reported that learner behavior actually worsened. At the end of the school year, two of the original thirteen educators hired by the first chief learner resigned.

In summer 2008, the chief learner resigned to accept another position within the district. Soon after, the district liaison who had worked with the educators the previous summer was appointed as the school's fourth chief learner in a little over two years. A district veteran, she was well positioned to mediate the tension between the mandate under which the school was founded and the environment in which it now operated. The district environment continued to shift as well. Philadelphia appointed a new CEO in February 2008—its third since SOF opened—bringing in a new leadership team and eventually reorganizing the regional structure.

As the school prepared for its third year, the chief learner had two priorities: establishing a positive, orderly school climate, and creating greater "transparency and transferability" between SOF and the district. During the fall semester, the chief learner implemented several staffing changes, including appointing a new dean to maintain a schoolwide discipline policy and to promote a positive climate with an emphasis on prevention. The new dean focused explicitly on supporting educators who were confronting behavior problems in their classrooms, creating an in-house suspension program for the most disruptive learners and contacting parents whenever difficulties occurred.

Toward the end of the semester, the chief learner presented a plan for the remainder of the year to the faculty. The message was twofold. First, it reaffirmed a commitment to the basic vision for the school and its mandate to be innovative. Second, it stated that the school needed to rethink its approach to realizing that vision. To do so, she argued, SOF first needed to implement stable, consistent systems and practices that were transparent (understandable) and transferable (compatible) with the rest of the district. In the short term, this meant accepting a greater degree of district involvement in the school's affairs. Specifically, she explained, the district had mandated adoption of certain elements of its instructional system, including the secondary core curriculum, weekly assessments of student progress in reading and mathematics, and a conventional, ten-period schedule similar to that used by other high schools. The challenge for the chief learner was to try to reconcile the tension that had emerged between the school's vision and district policy and procedure:

> Because we sit inside of a larger conglomeration, it is difficult to operate outside of the status quo. We realize that we may indeed have to design two reporting mechanisms for student achievement. One that will speak and connect to the district's information management system and [be] understood by colleges and universities and one that will accommodate our educational program. Because they didn't do that initially, it created a lot of problems for this organization.

While changes in leadership clearly influenced the direction of the school, so too did looming accountability pressures. Whether the school had deliberately moved toward increased transparency and transferability, spring 2009 marked the first time that SOF learners would take the PSSA and thus generate performance data comparable to other schools in the district and state. This presented multiple challenges. First, the school did not have traditional grade levels, and the different iterations of project-based assessment did not offer a clear mechanism for determining grade-level equivalence. It therefore proved somewhat difficult to determine who was, in fact, in eleventh grade and thus required to take the test.

Second, until the third chief learner was appointed principal, the curriculum had focused little on test preparation, or even on covering the material on which learners would be tested. With the school under increased scrutiny, there was a growing concern that poor test performance would further undermine its autonomy. Many educators saw the return to the core curriculum as essentially a test-preparation strategy.

By spring 2009, a notable shift had occurred at SOF. There was more order in the building, both in terms of consistent discipline and a common curriculum, instruction, and assessment. Instead of a curriculum organized solely around projects, learners now worked on projects two periods per week, with educators given considerable latitude in designing them. The chief learner stressed that the core curriculum was intended to be more guide than script:

> It is the floor, not the ceiling. Use it as a guide to needed content. You should be somewhere around where the planning and scheduling timeline says you should be. You still have a lot of leeway in terms of how you want to deliver it. I'm using the core as a safety net, if you will, to ensure mandated content delivery until our model is completed and can be implemented and executed with maximum fidelity. We're not starting from scratch. The genesis already exists. The core will allow staff to work at a healthy pace without worrying about creating projects for current learning.

In the chief learner's terms, SOF had "taken a step backward in order to move forward." The vision for the school, she suggested, remained the same as the day it opened, and she articulated it in terms similar to the language of the original design documents:

> The overall vision is to be able to create an instructional delivery model that allows students to create a learning path that will take them through to graduation. There will be what I will call a menu of pedagogical strategies where a student can say, "Okay, this is the content that I have to take in year one." I don't even want to talk in terms of year one, two, three or four. The learner will decide the length of the journey, the instructional strategies, and the models of assessment. The learner will be presented with the mandated courses, interdisciplinary projects, and standards, but will decide how he or she will demonstrate the mastery of the standards in the courses based on

the menu. Learning will be student centered and student driven, infused with inquiry and discovery every step of the way.

On balance, the faculty was supportive of the chief learner, but for different reasons. As a longtime partner of the school, she enjoyed a good relationship with the educators and a high degree of credibility as someone committed to the school. Some on the faculty, including many of the educators hired that year, agreed with her assessment that greater consistency and conformity were needed:

> I think the school started out to be revolutionary, but the world wasn't revolutionary. We still have to be able to let these students to go to a college and compete [for] scholarships. If we don't have a grade for them that shows that . . . if they don't have that GPA, they can't compete for the scholarships. And it's taken a step back, and now it's become evolutionary.

Others accepted the chief learner's plan because they perceived that she was responding to district pressure to conform and had limited influence over the school's direction. For this group, the return to a more conventional instructional approach felt like a departure from the school's vision. Rather than a step back to move forward, this group of educators saw the changes as a first step in a regression to a traditional high school model.

> So it's like before we were kind of pursuing projects, and now we're pursuing preparing for a test . . . This is such an amorphous environment, just because of the freedom that we had and now this transition into turning into a school like everywhere else in the district. It's all because there's immense pressure for improvement, for AYP, to pass the tests.

While the story of leadership at SOF unfolds over a three-year period, it is in many ways a story of three "first years." Each year began with a new CEO, a new chief learner, several new educators, and different strategies for organizing teaching and learning. While this presented considerable challenges, it also offers important insights about the role of leadership in catalyzing and sustaining innovation.

LEADERSHIP FOR INNOVATION

The role and impact of leadership at SOF is best viewed through two related frames. The first focuses specifically on the chief learner's role, while the second considers leadership at different levels of the system. The latter is critical because the story of SOF suggests that district leadership powerfully influences the options and strategies available to chief learners, and those strategies in turn affect relationships between chief learners and educators.

The Role of Chief Learner

Taken together, the experiences of the school's four chief learners offer a composite image of what effective leadership at SOF might look like. First, it must be empowering. Unlike many reforms, SOF is not a model to be implemented; it is a set of ideas to be realized. The daily work of bringing ideas into practice falls primarily on the educators, which requires tremendous effort, commitment, and creativity. To do this work, educators need autonomy to develop, test, and refine instructional approaches. Empowering leadership was a defining characteristic of the school in its first year, a period characterized by close collaboration and a remarkable investment of time and effort. When leadership took a turn toward a traditional monitoring and management approach midway through the school's second year, morale suffered and the school became more fragmented.

Second, leadership must be supportive. SOF is an experiment. Although carefully conceived, its evolution has raised dilemmas of organization and practice, and there have been setbacks along the way. Supportive leadership allows room for both risks and mistakes, while helping educators cope with the complexity of simultaneously developing and implementing a new educational approach. The first chief learner viewed setbacks—lessons or projects that missed the mark or struggles with individual learners, for instance—as part of the learning process. In her view, creating a continuous, relevant, and adaptive learning environment required such setbacks. The fourth chief learner faced different circumstances than her predecessors at both the building and district levels, but she went out of her way to mentor educators who were new to SOF. She also conveyed that while the district was assuming a more assertive posture toward the school, the work of the educators was valued and would be critical to future success.

Third, leadership must maintain organizational coherence. Empowering and supporting educators does not mean that there should be no school-wide norms, systems, or practices. An effective leader must know when divergence and even conflict are productive—that is, when they facilitate educator and student learning—and when they are not. To be sure, this is a fine line. Under the first and second chief learners, it appears that instruction may have become too decentralized, with learners having markedly different experiences depending on the educator team to which they were assigned. The educators themselves recognized this, moving steadily toward a more consistent approach to projects during the school's second year. The process unfolded without guidance from the chief learner, however, which was controversial and contested among the faculty. In such instances, the SOF experience suggests that the chief learner has a critical role to play in establishing common practices across the school.

Fourth, leadership must facilitate organizational learning. The successes and challenges of the first year at SOF arose in no small part from the fact that the chief learner and educators were constantly tinkering, revising, and reinventing schedules, curricula, staffing, and assessment. Consumed with inventing and reinventing, the staff had little time to institute systems or procedures that would formalize this process. Beyond the general scope of their teaching, there was almost no formal delineation of roles and responsibilities among educators. Aside from the original design documents, there were few formalized processes to orient and train newly hired educators. The absence of such systems was less a problem when the chief learner and educators were all of a single cohort and shared a common experience. When those dynamics shifted, however, the school had little on which to fall back. At no time was this more apparent than in the school's second year. Educators in the building assumed a variety of roles, and within their teams they exercised considerable control over traditionally administrative domains such as discipline. Yet none of these responsibilities was formally recognized or defined. When the third chief learner was hired, this resulted in conflicting expectations about work roles.

It is encouraging that these four characteristics of effective leadership all figure prominently in the education competencies used by Microsoft and the school district to hire both chief learners and educators. For example, competencies associated with empowering and supportive leadership include strategic agility and innovation, valuing diversity, managing relationships, motivating others and helping them develop, integrity and trust, and listening. Competencies associated with organizational coherence include organizational ability, setting priorities, directing others, and managing through processes and systems. Leadership for organizational learning is reflected in competencies such as decision quality and problem solving, learning on the fly, dealing with ambiguity, and managing and measuring work.

Still, the education competencies led to the appointment of very different chief learners. This might suggest that while the education competencies were comprehensive, they did not allow for differentiation among skills and attributes that were indispensable and those that were merely desirable. Another explanation is that shifting district priorities placed different demands on the school and thus created a need for different qualities in its chief learner. It could be argued, for instance, that both the first and fourth chief learners were "right" for the job. Each articulated a similar vision for the school, but the fourth was much more attuned to how the school would interface with the district and made a priority of strengthening those connections. This illustrates one way in which the characteristics and practices of effective chief learners are influenced by leadership at other levels of the system.

Leadership across System Levels

Important as it is, the chief learner position does not exist in a vacuum. What chief learners do is profoundly shaped by whom they work with, at both the district and classroom levels. The case of SOF shows how changes in district leadership can dramatically alter expectations of the chief learner and how, in adjusting to district changes, chief learners must also renegotiate their relationship to the staff in their own building.

It is hardly surprising that high turnover in district and school leadership presented challenges at SOF. Stable leadership is often cited as one of the key factors in maintaining a vision for change, which, in turn, is key to successful reform.[11] This was especially critical at SOF, where the school's vision was radically different from the way the district—indeed, most districts—typically approached high schools. This divergence was less apparent during the planning process and in the school's first year. It was understood by district leaders that SOF would chart its own course, even if this meant working outside district norms and systems. This expectation changed with changes in district leadership. Over the following two years, district leaders became more concerned with the degree of "transferability and transparency" at SOF, and a fundamental tension emerged. On the one hand, the school had been established with a mandate to innovate, and those who taught there were invested in that process. On the other hand, to align the school more closely with its systems, the district mandated adoption of a more conventional schedule and curriculum, which was a challenge to both the school's autonomy and its instructional model.

Each chief learner took a different approach to resolving this tension, which resulted in varying degrees of alignment and collaboration between themselves and educators. The first worked closely with the faculty but was less attentive to external relations with the district. The third aligned with the priorities of the district, resulting in conflict and tension with the faculty. More than any of her predecessors, the fourth chief learner sought a middle way, taking steps to quell district concerns and align with its systems while trying to assure the faculty that her commitment to the original vision remained. In each case, the work of the chief learner—what each prioritized and how they spent their time—was influenced by their relationship with district leadership.

Similarly, the extent to which educators at SOF played leadership roles, and the precise nature of those roles, was influenced by changes in both district and school leadership. The first year was highly collaborative, with the development of projects driving school organization and educators taking on administrative tasks as the need emerged. The second year began with the faculty filling the leadership void resulting from the first chief learner's resignation, but this changed dramatically when the third chief learner sought to redefine the role of educators along much more conventional (and subordinate) lines. In the third year, educators were again encouraged and supported in leadership roles, but their autonomy was circumscribed by district mandates.

The SOF conception of leadership as articulated in the original design documents was primarily focused on educators and learners. To some extent, it was also concerned with effective parental and community engagement. Far less evident in the original design was the role of the chief learner as the representative of, and advocate for, SOF within the district. This lack of focus on the more mundane, bureaucratic, and perhaps political aspects of leadership outside the building may not have seemed necessary when SOF was being planned. The school had strong support from district leaders and was granted broad license to chart its own course. In many respects, it was an idealistic view of educational leadership, and the work of both the chief learner and the educators reflected this entrepreneurial, inward-facing view. Under less than ideal conditions, however, it became clear that being creative and entrepreneurial were not the only skills needed to steer SOF from vision to action. In hindsight, paying greater attention to the ability to communicate and build relationships within the wider system may well have reduced the school's vulnerability to district change.

LESSONS LEARNED

While the case of SOF—with four chief learners and three CEOs in three years—is clearly an extreme one, leadership turnover is the norm rather than the exception in large urban school systems.[12] Similarly, the tension between individual schools seeking to innovate and the gravitational pull of the districts they inhabit is well known. Charter schools, for example, were introduced for the express purpose of piloting innovative approaches to schooling, yet the vast majority closely resemble traditional schools in their organization and instructional systems. Borrowing from institutional theory, Henry Levin refers to this phenomenon as isomorphism—the tendency of organizations to conform to the norms and structures of those institutions from which they derive legitimacy.[13] With SOF, Microsoft provided the design inspiration, but ultimately—and by design—the fate of the school lay in the hands of the district.

Experimental schools and the districts they inhabit have different mandates and different ways of assessing their effectiveness. At SOF, for example, the school was focused on developing a learning environment that was continuous, relevant, and adaptive, while the district was focused on making adequate yearly progress. These goals are not mutually exclusive, but they do imply different priorities. Districts focused on improving performance seek to implement and scale-up interventions with a proven record of success. By definition, schools such as SOF have no such record. Their development is not a process of replication guided by fidelity to a model, but rather of trial and error, experimentation, and reflection. And like all new ventures, they experience setbacks and make mistakes.

How can innovation be sustained in the face of institutional constraints and divergent mandates? The SOF experience underscores the importance of clearly defining and communicating the role of leaders and the scope of their influence at both the school and district levels. To fully realize the SOF vision, district leaders, chief learners, and educators have distinct yet interrelated responsibilities. To promote and sustain innovative school concepts such as SOF, leaders should consider several critical steps.

First, district leaders need to define the boundaries within which schools are free to innovate and chart their own course, while clearly and consistently communicating those boundaries both within the district and to the school. These boundaries should clarify any elements of the district's curriculum, instruction, or assessment systems that are nonnegotiable. While the need for boundaries might seem counterintuitive, the story of SOF suggests that they are vital. Absent clear, shared expectations about the school's autonomy relative to the district, the relationship between them underwent constant renegotiation amid leadership turnover.

Second, district leaders and their partners should determine how and when progress will be measured. These measures must be consistent with the school's vision. District leaders should also consider how school-level measures relate to systemwide progress indicators. In some cases they may be identical, while in others it will be necessary to identify analogues. At SOF, for instance, interim assessments aligned with a core curriculum and pacing calendar may not be conducive to thematic, project-based work. A more appropriate strategy might be to let the school determine both the timing and content of interim assessments and monitor its progress on its own terms. Given clear guidance from the district, school leaders should focus on getting the most out of their people and facilitating organizational learning.

Third, school leaders should work to support innovation within classrooms and collaboration across them. Educators should be encouraged to develop curriculum, pedagogy, and assessment tools and strategies that bring the school's vision to life. But equally important, they should be supported in sharing, revising, and adapting their approaches based on ongoing reflection and feedback from colleagues. A critical function of the chief learner is to create space for small-scale innovation while pushing for schoolwide consensus on effective approaches.

Fourth, the process of seeding innovation, monitoring progress, and sharing and interpreting feedback must be made systematic. School leaders play a critical role both in setting the expectation that this will occur and in developing tools and routines to support it.

Fifth, school leadership should organize and deploy resources around instruction. Teachers will be most empowered and effective if the school leader is able to mold the school's organization and resources around their instructional approach. Budgets, staffing, and schedules, in particular, should be driven by instructional needs rather than established conventions.

Finally, school leaders should conscientiously develop tools and processes to interface with the wider school system. They must be able to explain their work in language that is accessible to people outside of their organizations. This can be accomplished by relating measures of school performance with system performance, but it also requires school leaders to communicate the school's goals, organization, and progress with multiple stakeholders within the system.

It is interesting that the leadership lessons offered here focus more on organization, management, and communication than on instruction. This is not to suggest that leaders in innovative schools have no instructional role (though in the case of SOF, it could be strongly argued that instructional leadership resides first and foremost with the faculty itself). Rather, the story of SOF suggests that no matter how compelling a school's instructional vision, the vision cannot survive on its own. It is through these more mundane leadership functions—organization, management, and communication—that the vision can be cultivated and sustained.

WILL SOF LIVE UP TO ITS NAME?

To tell the SOF leadership story now is in some respects premature. After three years, the school is just catching its breath. It is clear, however, that SOF has reached a critical juncture. It has achieved a measure of stability, thanks in no small part to the dedication of the educators and the work of its current chief learner. The school has also improved communication and coordination with the district and established systems and processes to govern its work. Yet many of the founding principles of the school, such as the commitment to a continuous, relevant, and adaptive learning environment, were less evident in the school's third year than they were in its first. There remains a risk that, in an effort to adjust to district needs, the school will compromise too much of what made it the "School of the Future" to begin with.

Will the district allow SOF to resume the work of innovation, or will it assert greater control and thus draw it back into the mainstream? As the third year at SOF drew to a close, there were reasons for cautious optimism. For the first time in its brief history, the school will begin a new year with the same chief learner and CEO as the previous year. At a meeting with the faculty, the district's chief academic officer acknowledged that the school's needs around curriculum and assessment would and should be different from those of other high schools. Going forward, she encouraged the school to build on the curricular and instructional approaches that it had developed in prior years and committed district curriculum and instructional staff to support that process. The extent to which these sentiments are carried out in practice will profoundly affect the future direction of the school. With stable leadership and district support, SOF may yet have the opportunity to live up to its name.

5

Engaging Parents
and Community

Patrick McGuinn

THE VISION FOR School of the Future contained a number of innovative elements that were intended to create a new template for urban school reform that could be replicated across the country and around the world. Central to SOF's efforts to improve the academic performance of students from the predominantly minority and overwhelmingly poor neighborhood of West Philadelphia was a plan to engage students, parents, and community members more directly in the school's activities. A large body of academic research has established a positive connection between parental engagement and student achievement.[1] Recent research has also found that incorporating community work into the school curriculum—through service learning or volunteer requirements, for example—can be an effective pedagogical technique.[2]

At SOF, an innovative project-based curriculum and a state-of-the-art school facility—designed with community needs in mind and embedded with the latest technology—was to be the lynchpin of an effort to connect parents to the school and the school to the broader community. The SOF mission statement declares that "we want this school of the future to play a vital role in the community. We insist that it be integrated into the very fabric of community life." In particular, the statement calls for "true accessibility by nearby residents for community events and activities, adult education programs and training courses in the latest technology for families in the area, [and] new recreation facilities for this neighborhood." It also proclaims that "we are prepared to play an active role in the residential and commercial revitalization of this community."

This chapter traces the design and implementation of these efforts from SOF's opening in September 2006 to the conclusion of its third year in spring 2009. The original vision for the school still holds considerable promise and is widely supported by students, parents, and educators. To date, however, SOF has had only limited success in making this vision a reality in the area of parental engagement. It has had greater success in the area of community engagement, where several productive partnerships have been formed, but has struggled to systematically integrate service learning into the curriculum.

Three major challenges seem to account for this outcome. The first relates to student demographics: whereas SOF aspires to be a "break-the-mold" school, it nonetheless has had to confront the many socioeconomic disadvantages faced by all poor urban communities, which tend to produce low levels of student and parental engagement. The second has to do with the specific leadership and management context in which SOF operates: tremendous turnover in leadership at the school and in the district has posed a fundamental challenge to all the school's goals. The third challenge is political and bureaucratic: urban school districts tend to be organized around a hierarchical command-and-control system that centralizes and standardizes most educational policies in ways that stifle school-level flexibility and innovation.[3]

PARENTAL ENGAGEMENT

The original design of SOF contained grand aspirations for parental engagement. In particular, it promoted itself as an "open school" where parents would be a regular presence on site and intimately involved in school governance. For this to happen, however, two essential conditions first had to be met: administrators and educators had to be receptive and encouraging of such engagement, and parents had to be willing and able to embrace the opportunity. During the first three years of SOF, these conditions generally appear to have been absent, and efforts to reach out to parents were further complicated by logistical and technological challenges. One administrator noted that "the parental involvement piece is the most challenging issue for the school—many parents are not engaged at all." It appears that this situation is due to a combination of parental apathy and lack of time, insufficient outreach by the school, and cumbersome district policies. As a result, parental engagement at the school has not come close to reaching the original ambitious level laid out in SOF's mission statement, although some promising developments have occurred in recent months.

The school got off to a good start in reaching the broader community when parents and nonprofit groups became intimately involved in the search for its first chief learner and its initial faculty. One educator noted that she was impressed to find a parent helping interview her for her position, and that SOF's emphasis on parental and community engagement was a big selling point in her decision to join the school. Ultimately, however, she was disappointed to find that "the notion of an open school—and the resources to support that—have not really happened as advertised." A parent observed similarly that "for the first two years, the SOF was not interested in working with parents."

Why did SOF fail to live up to its expectations in these areas? This stemmed in part from a lack of sustained outreach from the school. One administrator commented:

> We had a very naïve feeling at the beginning that because SOF was new and exciting, parents would naturally get involved, but this didn't happen. We had higher expectations than we should have and we didn't focus on parents initially—we just assumed that engagement would happen on its own. But we ultimately found that generating parental involvement is more difficult than we thought it would be and that our parents face all of the challenges that urban parents elsewhere experience.

The class of 2010 at SOF has the following demographics: 98.4 percent are minority, 95 percent are from low-income families, and 14 percent have special needs.[4] The challenges that poor urban students face are considerable, multifaceted, and well documented in the urban education literature.[5] They include high rates of single parenting, drug use, and poor nutrition; low levels of parental education and involvement; and a lack of educational resources—books, computers, software, etc.—at home. The original planners of SOF were aware of the traditionally poor level of parental engagement in urban public schools and hoped to overcome it with an extraordinarily talented and committed faculty, a project-based curriculum, and the deployment of new technology.

TECHNICAL DIFFICULTIES

Interviews with SOF educators, administrators, and parents revealed that the school's efforts to engage parents were centered on a Web-based learning portal intended to provide students, parents, and educators with an unprecedented mechanism for communication and interaction.[6] Each student at SOF is given a laptop computer with the hope that, in tandem with the portal, it will increase the ability of students and their parents to focus on academic work and communicate with educators from home. Despite the partnership with Microsoft—the largest software company in the world—SOF has struggled to convert this vision into reality. The struggles to establish the portal as an effective tool for parental engagement have had two different sources: one technological and the other human.

Microsoft's high-profile affiliation with SOF created an expectation that its technical expertise would prove a major asset in the school's integration of educational technology. Perhaps surprisingly, however, it was not Microsoft that provided the initial installation, control, and support for the technology infrastructure but the Philadelphia school district's IT staff. This was a conscious choice by Microsoft and part of its broader effort to make the SOF model as replicable as possible. As Mary Cullinane, an education specialist at Microsoft, noted, "Our focus was on ensuring that we were integrated into the district and that this work didn't just become a Microsoft satellite office. We wanted to ensure that we learned from the challenges of doing it this way, as that would be how other schools around the country would have to do it." This arrangement, though, presented several challenges. First, for a school that aspired to be trailblazing in its use of technology, being wedded from the start to the same central office staff and technology protocols that supplied all the other schools in the district was an inauspicious beginning. SOF's reliance on PCs has also encountered technical integration problems with the district, which exclusively uses Apple computers and software.

In addition, the founders of SOF decided to emphasize "learning first and technology later" in its original design principles. While this may have made sense in the first year, it created problems later, when technology was to become more central to the school's approach to student instruction and its relationship with parents and community partners. As a result, the school did not have a full-time systems engineer until its third year, and progress on the development of the portal has been halting. During the school's first year, the portal was only used by students and educators. It was described by Microsoft's liaison at the school as "not very robust," and parents did not use it. One student remarked that "there have been lots of technical problems with the portal—it's not there when you need it." One of the primary purposes of the portal is to allow parents to easily and regularly monitor their children's academic progress and to ensure that they complete their homework. The school, however, initially struggled to find ways to make such information available to parents in a format that was usable and encouraged parents to utilize the portal.

REBOOTING THE PORTAL

The technical development of the portal—and the effort to integrate it more effectively into the life of the school—appears to have accelerated with the assignment of a Microsoft employee to serve as a liaison to the school on a full-time basis in spring 2008. In SOF's second year, a "beta version" of an enhanced portal was deployed, but parents reported that there were a number of software compatibility problems in trying to get computers to work with the school systems. Subsequent upgrades now permit students and parents to access homework assignments and educator comments, but technical complications with the portal continue. One feature of the site, for example, allowed students to upload their homework and parents to check whether the assignment had been turned in. But the portal only indicated whether a document—any document—had been uploaded, and it did not have the ability to verify that the document was in fact the work that had been assigned by the educator.

One educator noted that this loophole was exploited by students, including one who uploaded the same document fifteen times so that it appeared that she had completed all of her assignments. Further complicating the situation was that the project-based learning approach—involving multiple educators per project—and lack of traditional letter grades during SOF's first two years made it difficult for educators to clearly communicate student performance to parents. While the school has now converted to a traditional grading system, educators still cannot post student course grades to the portal due to privacy regulations, and parents have to use the regular district Web site to access this information.

SOF representatives indicate that many of the technical issues with the portal will be addressed in an updated version scheduled to be operational in summer 2009. The technical development of the portal, however, is only half the battle. For the portal to have a meaningful impact on parental engagement—and ultimately on student achievement—it must actually be used by educators and parents. Parents cannot access what educators do not post, and educators cannot use it to communicate with parents who do not log on. The educators at SOF do not seem particularly well positioned to take advantage of the portal. Surprisingly, for a school that was created to integrate technology from the ground up, SOF apparently does not use technological literacy as an explicit part of its criteria for selecting educators. While prospective educators must submit their applications online—thereby potentially weeding out candidates who do not have the most basic computer literacy—the experience or inclination to make use of computer technology is not a requirement.

The hiring process was further constrained by district human resources and union rules. Drexel University's Jan Biros, who participated in the development of SOF, observes in chapter two that this was severely limiting: "As I participated in the interview process, I was not confident that many of the teachers I interviewed had the creativity, pedagogical skills, or the technical ability to deliver the vision we had discussed and designed." In this situation, professional development at SOF took on even greater importance, but little training in technology or project-based learning appears to have been provided in the school's first year.

SOF also does not appear to have clear policies governing educators' use of the portal, and even where they do exist, educators report that the policies are not enforced. An administrator noted that the school requires, at a minimum, that educators post a class syllabus with assignments and due dates on the portal. By her estimate, however, approximately five of the twenty-five educators at SOF do only this minimal amount, and one educator admitted that even these expectations are not enforced. The head of the SOF Home School Association (HSA) noted that some of the educators at the school are not comfortable enough with the portal to use it. He estimates that at least 50 percent of educators do not use the portal with any regularity. One administrator identified six educators who have created "robust" class Web sites that use discussion boards and post class notes, videos of lectures, and online readings. Overall, portal use by the faculty appears to vary widely; some post information and use the site regularly, while others do so rarely or not at all. One student noted that "every teacher is on a different page; every class uses different amounts of technology."

As one educator observed about the portal, "The challenge is to get parents on it and to use it. We are dependent on the parents to use it and some do and some don't; like other urban school districts, we struggle with getting parents involved." Even many of those parents who are willing to make use of the portal, however, may lack the ability to do so. Several educators noted that a lot of parents at the school lack basic computer skills and that Internet service is not widely available. The original SOF mission statement indicated that the school would attempt to alleviate this problem by providing reconditioned computers to parents at a discounted rate, but such a program does not appear to have been attempted.

SOF has encouraged parents to use their children's laptops, which are provided by the school, but many children reportedly do not take them home, either because they do not plan to use them or because they fear that they will get damaged or stolen. In addition, while the school originally intended to take advantage of Philadelphia's unique program to create a free citywide wireless network (initiated in 2005), the city stopped funding the expansion and operation of the network in 2008. As a consequence, the availability and reliability of Internet access across the city is spotty (Philadelphia is among the least connected cities nationwide), particularly in poor communities such as West Philadelphia.

With the arrival of Tony Franklin from Microsoft in the spring of 2008, the effort to develop the portal and train educators and parents how to use it picked up steam. Franklin initiated a free portal-orientation session for parents at the school. By his estimates, however, while SOF has 380 students, only sixty to eighty parents have completed the training in the year and a half since it has been offered. A separate estimate put the total share of parents at about 30 percent. Whichever estimate is correct, it appears that at least 70 percent of parents have not yet received portal training. There also appears to be wide variation in perceptions of parental usage. Some of the students interviewed indicated that their parents made extensive use of the portal to access school information and get updates on their academic performance. One remarked that "our teachers and parents are connected and are in constant communication" and that "they are really on top of you."

On the other hand, one educator indicated that she "couldn't think of any parents that were using the portal this year." Another educator noted that only one of sixty-five parents in the school's second cohort had actually logged on to the portal, and one reported that only ten of ninety parents of students in her classes had ever logged on. It appears that the low usage rate was due partly to a lack of effort by the school to promote parental use, and partly to the fact that the portal contained little useful information. Several observers cited a steep learning curve with the portal for educators, parents, and students, and called for additional training. Figure 5.1 demonstrates both the limited use of the portal by students, parents, and educators during SOF's first year and the considerable increase during the 2008–2009 school year.

In the absence of a well-functioning and regularly used portal, it appears that the most common method of communication between SOF parents and educators are those used by the more traditional schools in the district: phone, e-mail, and the district Web site (for grades). In this sense, SOF has come to rely largely on preexisting technology to engage parents. Ironically, one parent noted that the portal seemed to actually *reduce* the frequency of educator and administrator communication through other, more direct methods, such as phone calls. Thus while the portal was intended to supplement traditional forms of communication, it may in practice have

FIGURE 5.1
Portal usage 2006–2008

YOY Comparison

	2006	2007	2008
Number of Class sites	↓ 3	↗ 58	↑ 200
Number of Mysites	↓ 0	↑ 335	↑ 411
Planner/Assignment Engine (SLK infused)	↓ 0	↗ 68	↑ 386
Storage used (documents, content)	4GB	7GB	Unk
Number of Learners	170	286	386
Number of Educators	13	19	26
Number of parent/extranet accounts	50		226

Source: Data provided by Tony Franklin, solutions specialist, Microsoft Innovation and Business Development Team, SOF, May 11, 2009.
Note: Class sites are individual sites managed by educators. Mysites are individualized per user—learner or educator. Assignments are generated individually by educators and distributed through the portal.

had the opposite effect. The technical problems and low parental usage led one educator to conclude that "the portal seems like more of a gesture than an effective tool."

Many people at SOF remain optimistic about the "enormous potential" of the portal to facilitate increased parental engagement and improved student performance. One educator said that "the portal is frustrating from the usability piece. I wish I could will it to work but it is being built as we use it. But ultimately it will be great and the key to everything we will do." While the SOF portal appears to offer considerable promise, it seems as yet largely unrealized. The degree to which the portal ultimately delivers on its innovative promise will likely be due to the efforts of the full-time, on-site Microsoft staffer—a support that is unlikely to be scalable if the SOF model is replicated.

HOME-SCHOOL RELATIONSHIPS

Beyond the portal, there are more old-fashioned ways that parents can be engaged at SOF, although one educator noted that "parents are hardly in the building at all." In addition, one parent noted that "what makes a good school great is the quality of the parents, but when the parent population is uneducated and has its own problems, then that carries forward. They just aren't able to sustain involvement in the school with all of the other things going on in their lives." Some parents also acknowledged that many other "parents haven't organized enough to be influential" and that "most of the parents at the school aren't mature enough" to be involved. Many of the kids at SOF, they observed, are essentially "raising themselves." They describe most parents as "not having the right attitude to get involved, . . . not providing much support for their kids, and not focused on their learning."

One parent observed that the school does not communicate regularly with parents, which is "one of his biggest concerns about the school." Indeed, there was not even a Home School Association at SOF during its first two years—an absence that is striking for a school that hoped to facilitate deep parental engagement. The first chief learner reportedly did not want traditional parent organizations, preferring a looser, less structured, and more democratic approach to parental involvement. But the parents I spoke with reported that the school did not seem interested in promoting parental engagement or even in receiving their input during the first two years. They noted that a lot of roadblocks existed, and also expressed anger and confusion about the leadership turnover, saying that "the second principal was a bust" and that "after the second year, parent leaders were spent and frustrated."

Parents and educators came together to hold meetings and elections for establishing an HSA during the fall of SOF's second year, but this effort was declared illegal by the regional HSA for having violated the group's procedures, which state that educators cannot be present for HSA board elections. An HSA was finally created during the school's third year, but as one leader remarked, "It has been a real struggle to get parents to participate." While eighty-one parents initially signed up to join the HSA, turnout at the monthly meetings has been poor. The March 2009 meeting had the best turnout so far, but only fifteen parents attended. One HSA leader estimates that only 20 percent of parents are involved in the school at all and only 10 percent are involved in any regular, sustained way. The HSA has formed six volunteer committees to work on various issues at the school, but their efforts are mostly focused on policies related to discipline, safety, tardiness, and cell phone use, rather than on academic concerns.

The constant leadership turnover at SOF has had a significant impact on the overall functioning of the school. This has been especially true when it comes to the pursuit of goals such as expanded parental and community engagement. The struggles that students and educators have had adapting to this constant turnover is well documented by Matthew Riggan and Margaret Goertz in chapter 4, but its impact on parental and community relationships has perhaps been even more profound. Learners and educators are in the school every weekday but parents and community groups are not, and therefore they must rely on educators and administrators to disseminate information. Discussions with SOF educators and administrators, however, revealed that this kind of outreach was generally one of the first things to go when the school was struggling to adapt to new leadership and policies. As one educator noted, "The parental engagement piece has fallen by the wayside due to having to deal with constant crises."

COMMUNITY ENGAGEMENT

A central part of the SOF vision was for the school to benefit—and benefit from—its surrounding community. As one parent observed, "The role of the community groups is extremely important; the lack of resources in many students' homes means that there is a real need for outside extracurricular [activities]." In addition, the West Philadelphia neighborhood surrounding SOF is one of the poorest sections of one of the poorest cities in the United States. Part of the rationale for spending taxpayer dollars on the shiny new school with state-of-the-art facilities was to provide a physical and spiritual center for community renewal.

Community leaders, such as the director of the West Park Cultural and Opportunity Center, were intimately involved in the original design of the school. They served on the search committee for the first chief learner and for the original group of educators. While the central element in the SOF approach to expanding parental engagement is the learning portal, the key to its efforts to increase community engagement is a project-based curriculum. The school's founders aspired to create an interdisciplinary, "community-based learning environment" in which students and educators would use longer blocks of class time to engage in thematic, community-connected projects centered on "essential questions."

The school encountered a number of obstacles as it attempted to implement this vision, however, with one administrator noting that they had a difficult time defining what project-based learning actually meant. Students, parents, and educators concur that the approach was put into operation at SOF before the curriculum had been fully developed. Although a curriculum-planning committee met for over a year prior to the opening of the school, it does not appear to have produced any curricular documents to guide faculty work. One educator went so far as to say that "the school was not prepared when it opened; it wasn't even finished being built yet. The staff, leadership, technology—everything—was a mess. The teachers were given a lot of flexibility, but there was no curriculum or discipline and things fell apart, and we had to build a new system." The lack of a detailed scope and sequence was in part by design, as the school's founders hoped to create an environment in which educators, students, parents, and community partners could work collaboratively and creatively to develop a more organic curriculum.

Such a nontraditional approach placed great weight on leadership support and continuity and on the recruitment and training of certain kinds of educators. As a district school, however, SOF had to follow district personnel policies and abide by the stipulations of the union collective bargaining contract. The result was that most SOF educators came from within the district and were trained and experienced in traditional pedagogical and curricular approaches. In addition, the initial cadre of faculty at SOF was very young and inexperienced—the majority were either brand new to teaching or in their first few years in the classroom—and this presented its own set of challenges.[7] A second-year educator, for example, when asked why he had not yet engaged in any community projects in his classes, responded that "he was still trying to learn how to do my job as a teacher." Reinforcing this point, one administrator observed that SOF educators "wanted to think outside of the box but had very little experience or knowledge of what is inside the box. They were trying to build the plane while flying it at the same time."

Despite these challenges, one educator called the project-based curriculum "the biggest success story for the school so far" and noted that every single faculty member participated in a grant-driven project during the school's first year. A parent remarked that the potential of project-based learning is "immense" and that his daughter "learned without even knowing it," but that "it ultimately depends on who is developing it and for what purpose." The school's first chief learner—often referred to as "visionary" by SOF educators and parents—fervently believed in the approach, which appears to have energized faculty and students alike. She resigned for personal reasons after only a year at SOF, however, and subsequent leadership changed the academic curriculum and schedule back to a more traditional approach. This was a major source of frustration for SOF educators, many of whom had come to the school specifically to work with a project-based curriculum. One administrator remarked that the resignation of the first chief learner was "a major blow to what the school was trying to do."

After the first chief learner's departure, an interim chief learner was appointed by the district. This new chief learner, however, had recently retired from a traditional district school and had little experience with or understanding of project-based learning. After six months, in December 2007, the interim chief learner was replaced by a permanent chief learner who had been selected by the district. Parents and community groups were not invited to participate in the search, and, perhaps as a result of this, the new chief learner never appeared to gain the support of educators or parents. One administrator described her as simply a "poor fit," noting that her time at the school was acrimonious and unproductive. As a result, this permanent chief learner moved on after only eight months at SOF. The fourth—and current—SOF chief learner came from the district central office, where she had been deeply involved in the original planning of SOF. Her understanding of the mission and history of SOF—as well as her longstanding relationships with key stakeholders in the school, the community, and the district—brought hope of a new start.

LEADERSHIP TURNOVER

This new start, however, also highlights the extent to which the frequent leadership turnover at SOF delayed the school's development during its first three years. One community partner recollected that "every time the leadership at SOF changed, the conversation changed." As with parental engagement, there do not appear to be clear policies about the quantity and quality of community engagement that is expected. SOF does not mandate that students work in the community, which is a common practice in many traditional high schools across the country. One administrator observed that this was a conscious decision: "The idea was not to have a requirement, but to create the opportunity, competency, and propensity" for service. This less structured approach appears to have worked during the school's first year, when every class participated in a project of some kind, but one administrator noted that "with the different changes in school leadership, this fell by the wayside."

Turnover in district leadership also had a major impact on SOF. The school was originally established as a partnership between the district and Microsoft. At the time, district CEO Paul Vallas was a devoted supporter of the project and was intimately involved in the initial negotiations with Microsoft to establish the school. Even before it opened, Vallas promoted SOF as a model that could help reform urban education across the United States. As a result of his deep involvement, Vallas was willing to give SOF the additional resources and flexibility with which to pursue unique reforms. At the end of SOF's first year, however, the school was struck by a perfect storm of leadership loss that removed all three of its founding visionaries: its original chief learner had resigned; the supportive district CEO had left for New Orleans; and the head of the city's School Reform Commission had stepped down. As one SOF administrator noted, "Everyone who had supported the school was gone."

When Vallas was replaced by Arlene Ackerman, SOF administrators spoke of the need to "reconnect" with the central office, a process that clearly was as confusing and stressful as it was time-consuming. While SOF leaders report that Ackerman has been supportive of the school, several educators feel that she does not believe in the efficacy of small schools like SOF and that they have been given less support since her arrival. In any event, SOF does not appear to occupy a prominent place in Ackerman's broader vision for the future of the district.

STANDARDIZING INNOVATION

Under its new leadership, the district put pressure on SOF to standardize its curriculum and grading practices. SOF's use of a project-based curriculum in its first year apparently caused considerable consternation in the central office because it was unable to measure student progress by traditional means. SOF's unusual block scheduling and nontraditional grading and course credit system, for example, created complications for students who transferred out of SOF. One school leader acknowledged that "not enough thought or effort was put into making the SOF transparent and transferable. This has proven a major stumbling block, and after all of the changes in the district central office, the original plan is not okay anymore." It also became increasingly clear that many students required intensive remediation in basic academic skills before they could participate meaningfully in a project-based curriculum.

The arrival of a new superintendent and chief learner, the desire to establish a "proof of principle" for the SOF model, and the extensive national and international media attention focused on the school put considerable pressure on SOF to document student learning through comparable—that is, standardized—tests. As one observer inside the school put it, "They were forced to show progress with their test scores." The focus on standardized test results pushed educators, directly and indirectly, to abandon more creative pedagogical approaches in favor of test preparation. One educator observed that "as we have become more traditional and adopted a core curriculum, we've really lost our focus on project-based learning and community engagement." An administrator concurred that "the move to a core curriculum has squeezed out a lot of other, more creative stuff." As SOF lost its most ardent supporters inside the district central office, its initial discretion over its internal operations—such as its curriculum, scheduling, grading, and personnel—was rescinded. While the first chief learner and educators were "site selected," for example, later ones were chosen by the district with little input from SOF, its parents, or community leaders. This led to a disconnect between SOF's original mission and a sense of frustration and powerlessness among staff.

Even when they had the flexibility to move forward with the project-based curriculum, SOF educators and administrators quickly encountered the difficulty of finding and sustaining the right kind of community partnerships for their service-learning initiatives. One SOF administrator noted that while there was initially considerable interest in partnering with

SOF, it quickly became clear that many of the organizations were interested in partnering with Microsoft, not SOF. She reported that other groups primarily appeared interested in using free student volunteers to advance the goals of their organizations, rather than in advancing the educational interests of SOF or its students.

PROMISING PARTNERSHIPS

Despite these myriad challenges, SOF has developed some promising community partnerships, three of which seem to operate regularly on a school-wide basis. The West Park Cultural and Opportunity Center seems to best embody the kind of community engagement originally outlined in the SOF mission statement. The organization uses SOF facilities (which remain open until 10:00 p.m. every night) to provide a wide variety of afterschool academic, vocational, and cultural programs to community members, and to SOF students, for whom these activities are free of charge. They include literacy, art, exercise, and GED courses for community members. SOF has also created an artist-in-residence program that brings in local artists to work with students in their classes during the day. West Park has literally moved into SOF by establishing its headquarters inside the school.

The West Philadelphia Alliance for Children (WePac) operates a resource center at SOF (and at a number of other area schools) that provides counseling, career exploration, college preparation, and leadership development. WePac also helps coordinate a tutoring program with Villanova University called Learners Connect! in which undergraduates from the honors program provide academic tutoring to SOF students.[8] While Villanova provides tutoring in other Philadelphia schools as well, they see the partnership with SOF as unique and have committed more university resources there through two permanently funded graduate student assistantships, on site twenty hours per week. Learners Connect! began as a completely online tutoring program, but it was changed to an on-site, face-to-face program in the second year and later moved into SOF classrooms in response to low levels of participation.

Villanova reports that in that first year, nine of the thirty-nine tutors did not end up having any e-mail communication at all with SOF students. An internal report found that out of the thirty who did, "the number of e-mails sent between the tutor and all of their learners ranged from one e-mail to 41, with the average being 10 e-mails sent, . . . [and] most reported communication ended by the beginning of October 2007." An effort to bring SOF students to Villanova's campus in fall 2007 was ultimately abandoned due to district regulations on field trips, but twenty students made the trip in 2008. Villanova's assessment of the tutoring program concluded that "the constant flux of the administrative environment at SOF made it very difficult to establish a stable relationship with more faculty members than our two liaisons . . . Not having a secure relationship with the chief learner kept our program from being as firmly established as it might have been."

In general, community groups praise the location and facilities at SOF and their potential for community work, but said that they are "underutilized." WePac estimated that forty students—only about 10 percent of the SOF student body—currently participate in its afterschool programs. Students indicated that attendance at the tutoring sessions is optional and that "most students don't go." Both West Park and WePac acknowledged that they have struggled to get more students to stay after school to take advantage of the opportunities they provide and to sustain the involvement of participating students over the entire school year.

The community partners indicated that they are able to access the SOF portal and would enjoy being able to use it to communicate with parents, but that they "don't sense that parents are using it. Tools are only as useful as people are willing [and] able to use it." Community partners noted that an additional problem is one of resources: SOF is supposed to operate on a regular Philadelphia public school budget (in part because of resource constraints and in part to permit the SOF model to be more readily transported to other schools). But this means that SOF does not have any additional funds with which to pursue innovation, especially in its goals for expanded parental and community engagement. SOF administrators, for example, cited the need for a full-time staff position dedicated to promoting, funding, and assessing community and parental outreach. Educators currently must undertake these efforts on their own, and as a result, one administrator remarked that those who attempt community work are "wiped out" at the end of the year and often unwilling or unable to sustain partnerships that they have cultivated.

The central office has also declined to grant SOF waivers from district policies that obstruct community activities at the school. One community partner declared that there remains a "radical distance between SOF and the Philadelphia school district." One educator was able to secure a federal Learn and Serve grant, but they ultimately lost it and had to return some funds "because the district makes it too hard to spend the money." She noted that district policies make it difficult to take students off school grounds and into the community and that it takes at least three weeks— and sometimes months—to get district approval for such trips. The educator drew a contrast between the restrictions on SOF community efforts and the flexibility enjoyed by the Global Leadership Academy, a nearby charter school. One community partner concurred that "district policies conflict with the desire to create an open community school." While SOF is available for community use on weekends, for example, district policy requires that a security guard be present at all times but will not pay for it. In addition, community groups that want to use school facilities have to pay to do so. When an arts festival was recently held at SOF on a weekend, its organizers were charged a $1,500 facilities fee in addition to the security fee. Community partners indicated that these fees have prevented them from using the school as a local hub in the way it was originally envisioned.

Some programs—such as a community choir comprised of students and members of the neighborhood that met in the school on weekends— have been canceled, and the initial proposal for community members to use the school's athletic facilities has not materialized. When SOF was built, neighborhood residents whose children were denied admission to the school were told that their families would still benefit from its community programming. But today there is the perception that the original promises made to the local neighborhood about SOF have not been kept, which has directed a lot of frustration at the school from the community. As one community partner concluded, "The robust vision about community engagement at SOF has not been operationalized or realized."

Currently, students and educators participate in interdisciplinary mini-projects for one school period a day—the last remnants of the original project-based curriculum. One current project involves a production of the play *Dreamgirls,* which has brought a number of community members—including a hip-hop choreographer, someone from a local music station, and a lighting designer—into the school to work with students. The students presented the show in a performance open to the whole community at the end of the school's third year. Another community-based project, developed in an African American history class, has partnered with the Underground Railroad Museum at the nearby Belmont Mansion. Students in the class volunteer as docents in the museum, participate in historical reenactments, and develop educational materials. Another partnership involves the Eden Cemetery, the oldest African American–owned cemetery in the United States, and students are working to make the site's archives available to researchers and the public. A science class partnered with a group called Earth Force to have students plant native flora alongside the on-off highway ramps. Another class has partnered with a group at the University of Pennsylvania on an organic food project called Food Trust.

Despite these particular efforts, one educator observed that overall "outreach to the community has not gotten much traction." Another remarked that "the school did a lot of community engagement in its first year but not much since; where it exists now it is largely small and isolated." One veteran educator with extensive experience in service learning distinguished between "real partnering" with community groups and the kind of "touching" with community groups that she sees in many SOF classes. She noted that "unfortunately I've been . . . the only educator who has been really involved with community partnerships here." She remarked that she "feels extremely isolated and underused" and "dismissed" by younger educators at SOF, and that no one listens to her because "everybody here thinks they know everything already." "They want to create new things," she said, "[but] are reluctant to learn from the past, from the successes and failures of previous efforts." The young SOF faculty needs much more training in service learning, she observed, but despite having a grant that enables her to give educators a stipend to undertake such training, only three SOF educators have taken advantage of it.

Community partnerships are difficult to establish and sustain even under the best circumstances, but clearly SOF faculty and prospective community partners have not been operating under anything close to optimal conditions. Indeed, for much of the past three years, even the chief learner's support for community engagement was not a guarantee. The current chief learner has brought welcome stability and leadership to the school and, equally important, appears committed to the school's original focus on parental and community engagement. Still, she acknowledged that SOF "had to take a break and adopt a more traditional curriculum until we can develop a clear plan for reaching our goals." She recently convened a faculty meeting at which it was agreed that the school would begin to design a complete project-based curriculum for introduction in September 2010. One SOF parent concluded that "there is not a lot of outreach from the school to the community—maybe they want to make sure that everything in house works first."

CONCLUSION

The evolution of SOF over its first three years highlights the many challenges that face school reformers in urban districts. The students at SOF— like many in underprivileged urban areas—come overwhelmingly from poor, minority families and bring to school a wide variety of socioeconomic disadvantages. Several community and school leaders emphasized how difficult it is to engage parents and community partners in an urban high school and that SOF's efforts must be viewed in context. One observer argued, for example, that "SOF should not be held to suburban school standards," and that given the demographic challenges, if SOF is able to get 10 percent of parents and four or five community groups involved in the school, then that is a "great success."

SOF hoped to overcome these challenges through a project- and service-based curriculum and enhanced parental involvement made possible by new technology. But public schools—and particularly public schools in large urban districts—that aspire to be innovative must first secure and defend sufficient "entrepreneurial space." Reform is about innovation and experimentation, but district central offices are about standardization. As the leader of one SOF community partner observed, "The biggest challenge has been trying to create a unique school model within a traditional district. The district requirements are cumbersome." In chapter 8 of this volume, Mary Cullinane puts it this way: "Innovation swims upstream in the river of status quo."

Related to this bureaucratic challenge is a political one, since bureaucracies are controlled by officials who have their own agendas and constituencies. To experiment with costly and potentially risky reforms, urban public schools like SOF need the long-term support of district and city leadership. As SOF experienced firsthand, however, urban superintendents typically have an extraordinarily short life span (on average about two years) and the loss of an ally in the central office can have major consequences.[9] Microsoft and the school's founders chose to establish SOF as a comprehensive district high school under the control of the School District of Philadelphia. While this was intended to make the reforms as replicable as possible, it ultimately constrained how far SOF could advance the reforms. As Chester Finn notes in chapter 9, SOF was not given any "institutional mechanisms to vouchsafe the school's long-term identity," which made it particularly vulnerable to the vicissitudes of district politics. Ultimately, innovative school models like SOF may be better served by operating as charter schools rather than traditional district schools, given the former's greater freedom from bureaucratic regulations.

Like urban superintendents, urban principals often have short tenures. This presents a major management challenge, as effective and stable school leadership is crucial for the implementation of new reforms. SOF has had four chief learners in three years, and each brought not only a different leadership style but also a different educational philosophy. The constant internal turmoil at the school made it difficult for educators to focus on external relationships with parents and community partners. One community group leader noted that at SOF, "people talk about always being in crisis mode; it's hard [or] impossible to work on [a] long-range vision. There is no overarching commitment to community engagement."

Lessons Learned

What could SOF have done differently? What lessons emerge for school reformers? First, the history of SOF reinforces how dependent innovation is on charismatic, dedicated, and sustained leadership—what Joe Williams, executive director of Democrats for Education Reform, has called the "James Deans" and "the rebels *with* a cause" in American education.[10] There is a delicate balance, however, that innovative school leaders must strike as they try to change the rules while playing by them. The nontraditional background of the school's founding chief learner, who spent a decade at a private school in Italy before joining SOF, may have proven a detriment in this regard. It was hoped that her background would make her more open to innovation and willing to experiment. While this may have been true, her lack of experience and relationships in Philadelphia may have made her less able or willing to navigate the treacherous local bureaucratic politics.

The first chief learner's unexpected departure from SOF underscores another essential point for reformers. For innovation to truly take hold in a school and be implemented effectively over the long haul, it must be institutionalized. While the school leader plays a crucial role, innovation cannot be dependent on individual administrators or educators, it must be embedded in the school's organizational culture.[11] Every employee at the school must understand its mission and be committed to pursuing it.[12] This has not been the case at SOF; since district human resources and union policies constrained the eligible applicant pool, some educators were not site selected, and the leadership itself has often veered from the original mission and pedagogy of the school. In addition, SOF founders' and educators' desire to create an organic and flexible climate for curricular innovation led them to discount the importance of creating a scope and sequence to guide teaching and learning. (In general, administrators concede that documentation has been spotty at the school, which has exacerbated the impact of the leadership turnover.) The school's focus on being innovative and distinctive also seems to have led founders and educators to learn insufficiently from the successes and failures of previous attempts at urban school reform—and, in particular, other attempts to increase parental and community engagement—elsewhere in the United States.

In sum, it is nearly impossible to assess the efficacy of SOF's approach to parental and community engagement and the project-based curriculum and learning portal intended to bring them about because the approach has been implemented only partially to date. SOF has had an extraordinarily tumultuous first three years. While it is clearly too early to speculate about its long-term prospects, and despite the development of some promising community partnerships, to date SOF serves more as a cautionary tale than a model to be emulated. Turnover in school and district leadership has generated enormous instability, confusion, and mission change. A third-year student commented that "there has been so much drama here that you would have thought School of the Future was the school of the past."

Ambitious expectations for parental and community engagement have been dashed by an inability to overcome the many well-documented obstacles—such as high rates of poverty, crime, and single parenting, combined with low achievement and computer use—that plague urban schools across the United States. Collectively, these challenges have prevented SOF from implementing its innovative model effectively and from realizing its grand ambitions. As one SOF parent observed, "Project-based learning is not really happening. Parent-educator communication is not really happening. The school has the right ideas—they sound great—but right now they are mostly superficial. We need to get real about this, to make the ideas work in practice." Even the current chief learner acknowledged, "I don't think that we are that different from other schools yet."

Back to the Future

Fittingly, however, the future appears brighter for SOF. Microsoft's commitment to a full-time staff member to provide on-site technical development and the appointment of a new chief learner who is committed to the school's original vision appears to have SOF poised to move forward—both as a school and as a potential reform model for American education. As one SOF student asserted, "We are the lab rats; the school is still a work in progress. But there is lots of potential for the future, and it will work better for the students coming behind us." The current chief learner has brought desperately needed structure and stability to SOF. A redesigned learning portal that incorporates educator, student, and parent feedback will launch this summer with enhanced functionality, and the school has initiated a more comprehensive training program to facilitate its use by all three groups.

SOF has also returned to site selection of its new cohort of educators, and they are being interviewed by a diverse team of stakeholders—students, educators, parents, community partners, and Microsoft advisors—using the corporation's personnel protocols.[13] In March 2009, the chief learner and faculty recommitted themselves to the school's original mission statement and to the development of a project-based curriculum, which they hope to have in place for the 2010–2011 school year. The school also plans to require seniors to add a community-service component to their district-mandated senior projects. After three difficult years, SOF is returning to its roots—back to the future.

6

Teaching from Scratch

Standards, Technology, and Innovative Instruction

Dale Mezzacappa

FOR MANY OF THE educators who eagerly applied, working at School of the Future in Philadelphia seemed like a dream come true.

One young woman pursuing an education degree at the University of Pennsylvania drove by the building every day while it was under construction. She knew little about it, however, until one of her professors talked about what had gone into its conception and design. Hooked by the vision, she said, "I just started stalking the school, for want of a better word."

"It was presented as a school that is trying to fix education," said the native New Yorker, who has a dual major in cognitive science and economics and was getting certified in both social studies and math. Her student teaching at a nearby Philadelphia comprehensive high school, with a dropout rate that exceeded 50 percent and a spot on the state's list of dangerous schools, had convinced her that the "school system in this country was broken. I know it sounds grandiose, but the whole point [of SOF] is to do things a different way because clearly the old way wasn't working."

Another young man, who majored in computer engineering and philosophy at Drexel University, was getting his degree in math education at Temple University. He was also intrigued by the construction site he passed every day. "I read about the mission of this place, and I'm, like, that's perfect for me," he said. "I wanted to be part of something that was about changing education, about asking fundamental questions."

Older educators were attracted, too. "It was a better fit for what I was being taught for, science education for the future," said a chemist and military veteran who sought out a graduate program at the University of Pennsylvania to pursue teaching as a second career. A twenty-two-year Philadelphia teaching veteran said, "It sounded exciting, different, like it would be a challenge and a change. I like the fact that you can be creative. Here, the sky's the limit. Whatever you want to do, you can do."

The challenge for these and the other educators in the school's first three years has been to create a new educational paradigm while still answering to the demands of the old. Building SOF has been compared by more than one person to building an airplane while flying it. Those involved, however, discovered that the default educational model—organized around bell schedules, teaching separate subjects in isolation, the assumption that most students learn the same material in the same way, the lockstep progression through grade levels, report cards with letter grades, and other conventions that most of America understands as "school"—does not give ground easily.

In short, these educators have discovered that the sky is not the limit, even in a school as technologically advanced as SOF.

While trying to re-imagine education for the twenty-first century, which was the vision for this partnership between Microsoft and the School District of Philadelphia, SOF educators were hampered in some cases by inexperience or, conversely, by longstanding habits and practices. In other situations, they have been stymied by an impatient school district bureaucracy more intent on setting down requirements than finding ways to support the kind of wholesale innovation that the school was designed for. A huge blow came when the first carefully chosen chief learner left after just one year, plunging the school into a leadership crisis. Looming over all was the sheer difficulty of the task that Microsoft and the school district had set: creating a new, forward-looking, replicable model for the very students who have historically been the most ill-served by American education.

THE FIRST CRUCIAL DECISION

Unlike most of the other small high schools created during the administration of former district CEO Paul Vallas during his five years in Philadelphia, SOF is a neighborhood school, with learners chosen by lottery. There are no admission requirements, no test-score cutoffs. Microsoft insisted on it.

For some of the educators, especially the younger ones, this particular challenge was what drew them. They were hungry to help redefine what high school could look like for the typical student in a big urban school district.

"[SOF] was doing something about the problem rather than just accepting that the problem exists," said the young math and social studies educator whose student-teaching experience at a nearby comprehensive high school left her "feeling defeated." She thought such places were simply going through the motions of school while tacitly accepting that most students would leave ill-prepared whether they graduated or not. Another young educator who had also done her student placement at a neighborhood high school relished the chance to fix a system that was "just very broken."

Yet, this test proved greater than anyone had anticipated. Not only did most of the learners enter SOF with low skill levels in reading, writing, and math, as a rule they had experienced such top-down, prescriptive schooling that they had no clue how to take control of their own education in the way that was being asked of them.

"Most of the kids at [SOF] are like those at every other comprehensive high school, reading somewhere between first- and second-grade level and eleventh-grade level," said one Philadelphia school district official who was involved in the start-up. Some of the learners readily took to this new concept of school, but many did not. And while some educators believed that the breakthrough SOF model was what the learners needed to climb out of that rut—that the model itself was the best way to build skills—others were constantly pulled back by the thought that the learners first needed traditional instruction to fill in gaps in their backgrounds and knowledge.

"I could only imagine what it was like for the learners when they first arrived in this building," said one veteran Philadelphia educator hired the first year. "Everything's online for you. Your math's online. Your writing's online. Your foreign language is online. They were never taught like that. They needed gradually to be eased into this."

Several people involved in the school have gone so far as to say that there has been a culture clash between the design and expectations of the school and the learners' readiness to take advantage of it. "The leadership when we opened the building went into this with certain assumptions, and they were that the children . . . were coming already motivated to learn and were at a certain skill level. That was not the case," said one school official who has had several roles at SOF. "Had more thought been put into where these learners were coming from and what they were coming with, we may have realized a greater degree of success."

In short, the argument has been made that the learners weren't ready for this wholesale change. While it is certainly a fact that many of the learners came with low basic skills, the bigger truth is that in some ways, neither the school district nor Microsoft was ready for such change.

HIRING THE EDUCATORS

Microsoft had to mesh its advanced, highly personalized hiring method with the school district's antiquated and centralized one. Spawned in an era of rampant patronage and political favoritism, Philadelphia's system historically privileged seniority over all else and left little discretion to principals to choose their own teaching staffs. In the name of "fairness," it virtually removed human interaction from the process, ignoring this crucial step for building top-notch learning communities.

The seniority system was so embedded in the city's teacher culture that it was in place before the Philadelphia Federation of Teachers won collective bargaining rights in 1965. Each vacancy was filled strictly by the most senior qualified teacher who applied; even new educators—ranked in order of scores on a civil-service-type placement test—picked where they would work rather than having principals select them. The new educators started choosing from among the remaining vacancies after a musical-chairs transfer system for the veterans ran its course, delaying the process so far into the summer that many top candidates gave up and took jobs elsewhere.

Even as other big-city districts moved toward school-based hiring in the 1990s, Philadelphia stood firm. The first crack appeared in the 2000 contract, when the union reluctantly agreed to a plan in which schools could use so-called site selection, or on-site hiring of teachers, if two-thirds of the teachers voted to allow it. The union, however, didn't always facilitate the site-selection balloting, especially in schools considered desirable to veteran teachers. Four years later, just 44 of more than 250 schools had opted for it.

But in the 2004 contract negotiations, district leadership, particularly James Nevels, the chairman of the School Reform Commission (SRC), made site selection a priority. Nevels, tapped to lead the SRC when the state took over the Philadelphia schools in 2002, argued that modernizing hiring was the bare minimum necessary to convince elected officials and other stakeholders that the district was serious about change. "School reform without site selection is 'reform lite,'" he said at the time. "We're one bad contract away from being D.C., the worst urban district in America," referring to the troubled schools in the nation's capital.[1]

Nevels went public with his campaign during negotiations and ultimately won a partial victory: an agreement with the union that half of new vacancies would be site selected and half filled in the traditional manner.[2] Newly created schools, however—and district CEO Vallas was opening new small high schools by the handful—were allowed to choose all their teachers through site selection for the first two years. That crucial provision paved the way for SOF. To fulfill its vision, the school needed the ability to carefully select teachers with qualities that Microsoft and district leaders had determined were necessary to design, promote, and sustain educational innovation.

Not only was Microsoft's hiring system highly personalized, it turned on its head many conventional notions about what to look for in a teaching staff. Instead of basing its evaluation of a candidate primarily on what the person had already accomplished, the hiring process keyed in on behaviors. And beyond simply toting up credentials, this system was designed to elicit competencies—whether the person could, for example, learn on the fly, manage time, listen actively, motivate others, assess talent, build effective teams, cope with conflict, and deal with ambiguity.

Dealing with ambiguity was particularly important. In the envisioned learning environment, learners would exclusively work on interdisciplinary projects in a paperless school. To accommodate the projects, schedules would vary each day rather than be based on set periods for separate subjects. As a result, some of the critical questions asked about each candidate were very different than the norm in teacher hiring. Could this person be comfortable with the lack of traditional structure? At any given time, there might be a tour group coming through—could the person adjust to that? As with any technology, there would be days when the network was down—could he or she adapt without falling apart?

All told, thirty-seven competencies were deemed important for educators, divided into six categories: strategic skills, operating skills, organizational skills, individual excellence, results (action oriented), and courage (in assessing talent and conflict management).[3] That process had been used to find the chief learner and yielded a woman whose most recent educational experience had been at a private school in Italy—someone who by all accounts had expressed a view of education that was inspiring and visionary, in sync with Microsoft, and willing to work diligently to make it happen. She, along with Mary Cullinane, Microsoft's education director, and several school district officials, presided over hiring the first cohort of educators.

The goal was not necessarily to hire all moldable newcomers. "The competencies are not associated with any specific age," Cullinane said. Plus, it is hard to make blanket generalizations. Sometimes, she said, younger educators are whizzes at classroom management, while older ones quickly see how technology can accelerate the learning process. To find candidates,

Microsoft used the school district's limited recruitment outreach and took some additional steps, such as advertising heavily on the Microsoft Web site. But because it wanted to devise a replicable process, the team did not pull out all the stops. "We could have gone to the Department of Education in each state and asked, 'Who is your teacher of the year?'" said Cullinane. "We didn't do that purposefully. We had to take into consideration [our limited] budget and the resources other schools had."

The team set out basic criteria, including valid teacher credentials and dual certification, so that educators could fit into the project-based, interdisciplinary model. The process itself was designed to elicit the desired behaviors before the candidate ever met interviewers. There was no phone number in the ads, which required applicants to respond via the Web. "Immediately, someone not comfortable with that would probably deselect themselves," Cullinane said. Once the decision was made not to cast a nationwide net for top talent, the pool of people who met the criteria was relatively limited—perhaps fifty made it to the interview stage. Cullinane wasn't surprised. "We were looking for dual certification with a tendency toward project-based learning in a district where that is not as prevalent," she explained. Not to mention people who could integrate technology into the classroom and were comfortable being "in a brand new high school that everybody would be watching."

THE LOOP

Those who made the first cut first went through the "Loop," or sequential interviews, each designed to elicit information on a particular competency. The interviewers included the chief learner, district officials, community members, and a few high school–age students from West Philadelphia, all of whom were trained in what questions to ask. The chief learner also added questions of her own. "If my group was looking at writing skills or . . . classroom management skills, another group was talking about using technology with instruction," said a school district official. "Another group was asking questions related to composure or the ability to think on your feet."

Two thumbs down eliminated a candidate. Those who survived that gauntlet were then invited into a group activity, a roundtable in which they tried to solve a problem or plan an interdisciplinary project while others observed and made notes. Afterward, the entire observation group got together to discuss the applicants and make recommendations, but the final decision was left up to the chief learner.

The first chief learner explained her goals in hiring the faculty: she wanted people who would "walk the walk, talk the talk." She continued: "If we said to kids, 'You have to work in teams,' then we as educators had to be able to work in teams. If we said to kids, 'You have to resolve your differences in a productive way' . . . then we had to be able to do that."

Educators had different reactions to the hiring process. While some reported being discomfited, others said they appreciated what it was trying to accomplish. "I applied to fifteen district schools and charters, but none asked me to take out a personality assessment to find out what member of a medieval kingdom I would be," said one young educator. "We had to . . . talk about . . . how that affects who we are . . . in a classroom." Other applicants, though, declined to take the personality assessments.

The application also called for designing a project around content standards. "And that was totally different from any of the other schools [I applied to]," said one young educator. "It was clear to me that [SOF] was where I wanted to come." Another candidate, a veteran of the district, said she saw a subtext to the hiring gauntlet: eliminating the type of Philadelphia teacher who says, "My hours are nine to four, and that's all I'm going to do." Her hiring process spanned three days and involved three trips to district headquarters. "That alone weeded out individuals not willing to do that much," she said.

There were other considerations. The school district still follows an old consent decree requiring racial balance on all school faculties, but that was not the main reason for seeking a diverse staff.[4] Variety in race, age, gender, experience, and familiarity with the Philadelphia system was important in dealing with issues that would surface as the educators faced the day-to-day realities of their jobs.

Building a faculty this way clearly has advantages and disadvantages. It is certainly better than the hit-or-miss nature of Philadelphia's centralized, impersonal hiring process, which is largely controlled by the teacher's preferences, not district or school needs. Using competencies to judge a teacher's effectiveness—or potential effectiveness—is not the common practice in education. But judging applicants by competencies has a better chance to create a cohesive learning community. Involving teachers and people and students from the neighborhood in the selection process also has the advantage of helping to build community. And it is useful to break down the mindset that teaching is a solitary profession that requires minimal interaction.

One overarching problem in hiring teachers is that there is no standard evaluation and few outcomes-based criteria on which to judge performance. Simply considering paper credentials and experience often provides little useful information about whether a person is effective. At the same time, it is too early to say whether using competencies instead of more traditional criteria yielded a more effective faculty for SOF. However, the process did yield people with a variety of backgrounds. There were an African American, Jesuit-educated ex-Navy man who migrated from industry; a young white counselor just out of grad school at a local university; a longtime veteran of Philadelphia, who had come to teaching after working at nonprofits, including the YMCA, and had made service learning her specialty; and a recent University of Rochester graduate certified in both social studies and math.

In that first year, there were thirteen educators on staff, including the chief learner. And while the process was not deliberately skewed to find new educators, most of the new hires were either right out of graduate school and in their first job, or a relatively inexperienced career-changer. About one-third of them were traditionally trained, veteran Philadelphia teachers.[5] The care and complexity of the hiring process did lead to some problems in the first year. For one, the chief learner ran out of time before completing the staff, and some last-minute decision making was necessary. Jobs were offered, said one district official, to people who originally might not have been among the highest choices.

The process began anew in the spring of 2007. The second year was slightly different. The original chief learner still directed the process and educators and learners played a part, with the role of the district and Microsoft somewhat diminished.[6] As in the first year, the chief learner made the final decision. This time, of the eight new core-subject educators, six were brand new to teaching.

And then, in July, the chief learner resigned, abruptly and without much explanation. She informed the staff via e-mail. Many of the educators hired by her for the second year said they felt abandoned. "She hired me and then she left," said one, still visibly shaken by it all. "I was looking forward to working for her."

This led to a leadership vacuum that deeply affected the school's second year of operation and the hiring of the third educator cohort. A new chief learner, who would also stay a short time, followed the Loop hiring process, but she had her own ideas about whom to hire and why; she soon left for another position in the school district.

By this time, due to the school's chancy reputation within Philadelphia, there was no rush to work at SOF among senior educators, and some positions went begging as school was set to open in the fall of 2008. Some vacancies were set to be filled centrally because the right to full site selection had lapsed without a faculty vote, a necessity that had been overlooked in the turmoil of the second year.

One young educator explained how he was hired. After teaching Spanish for ten years in rural Delaware, he moved to Philadelphia for personal reasons. Not even sure he wanted to continue in the profession, he applied for a job in the school district "at the last minute." On the first day of the school year, he was told to come to the central office at a specific time to choose from among the remaining Spanish vacancies. Like the other new hires, he waited for his name to be called. Then he proceeded to a table where he was given a list of jobs for which he qualified. He had a minute or two to make a selection. This teacher, who knew nothing about Philadelphia, stared at the list of fifteen Spanish vacancies until rescued by an official from the teachers union, who saw that he had a master's in applied technology in education. She recommended SOF and he took her advice. But when he went to check it out, the staff was running around preparing for the learners' arrival. "No one knew that I had been hired," he said. His experience was a far cry from the careful, intensive, multistep hiring process considered crucial to assembling a cutting-edge staff. But, as it turned out, the fit was pretty good. "I love it here," he said.

By the fourth year, however, the hiring process had evolved into a model not just of site selection but of school-based decision making. The chief learner turned over the process to an educator who had volunteered for the task. This educator sent an e-mail to the entire student body and faculty inviting participation. Some twelve of the twenty faculty members and twenty to thirty learners—who were not screened for their behavior or achievement records—participated in interviews at some point, along with about four parents and one or two other community members.

The educator designed an online application process that required essays, blogging, and written integrated lesson plans. More than 200 people applied, 150 were invited to move to the next step, and 46 completed the online tasks and were invited in for the interviews and loop process. Of those, 12 were offered positions.

Lessons from the Hiring Practice

During the planning year, the schools' visionaries could have partnered more actively with local universities to jointly develop a training model based on the competencies. This could have been accessed by both new educators and veterans interested in a change. Other successful break-the-mold schools, including High Tech High, have essentially received state approval to license their own teachers. It could also have done more outreach beyond Philadelphia, at least in the initial phases.

Since the vision of the school's founders was for an educational environment so different from the experience of most educators—and most teacher education—it is incumbent on them to devise a more focused, structured, and continual professional development process that starts well before the teacher begins work and continues throughout their experience. And it should include forthright discussions of cultural differences and their educational implications.

BUILDING CURRICULUM

The intention for School of the Future was to build curriculum from the ground up, to make it organic, responsive to the needs and interests of the learners, and theoretically unfettered by either the school walls or the pages of a book. The learning was to spill out into the community, engage parents and others, and speak to the neighborhood's real needs. Schedules would serve the learning experience, not the other way around, and most instruction would be both interdisciplinary and individualized.

In an interview session with a new educator, who asked, after hearing that the curriculum would be ever changing, whether she would ever be able to teach the same unit more than once, the original chief learner explained the breadth and uniqueness of the SOF vision:

> No, because there's no way that the kids you have [the] next year or [the] next month are going to have the same needs, prior skills, or project trajectory as the kids you have now. I can't ever say that you will teach that unit again. You might teach parts of it, the things you learned about the planning or content might come up in various places. But, no, that particular lesson or unit that you designed is not something you get to do every September or every October, like you would at another job.

She added, "We're the School of the Future. You don't know what the future is."

This chief learner later explained that she was very opposed to educators acting as technocrats who taught what others told them to teach and weren't responsive to learners' needs: "School of the Future . . . wasn't just 'fix the edges,' or 'fine-tune this,' it was 'create a different kind of environment that would connect kids to learning, hook them in . . . adapt to them.'"

The implication of the nationally televised opening day for the new school was that the boldness of this vision would change schooling in

America, especially for urban students. Each learner was getting a free laptop. This was a paperless school; there was no budget for books. Learning would be internally driven, using everything technology had to offer. The watchwords—continuous, relevant, adaptive—drove the model.

But even on the first day, there were problems. Some educators had been brought on board at the last minute, so there hadn't been sufficient time for team-building. The learners arrived, entering a school (and building) different than anything most of them had ever experienced. They wouldn't exactly attend classes—going from math to English to science to history— on a set schedule each day. Instead, they would do projects. They would have their own computers, rather than notebooks and textbooks. There were three "learning cycles," not two semesters, each divided into two marking periods. Most educators had dual certifications and would work in teams, meaning that they could grade and evaluate the learners in more than one of the traditional subjects—English, math, science, and social studies.

It was exciting, ambitious, forward looking—and overwhelming—for both educators and learners.

"Educators wrote their own curriculum," said one of the brand new educators among the original faculty. "It was project based, mission and vision driven." Working in teams, they devised projects with the help of a Web exchange called Understanding by Design, which provides materials and helps educators develop interdisciplinary, project-based units that meet the subject-matter standards in each state.[7]

But older educators said that the professional development for both curriculum writing and use of technology was minimal. One said she got very little out of the Understanding by Design training. Individual teaching groups met together to forge their projects, but the entire faculty never got together to discuss direction and coordination. Some teams did more than others. "We never met as a staff and reviewed any of it," said one educator. "My group disintegrated . . . so it just became a matter of completing the assignments and hitting 'enter.' So there was nothing."

The young educator who had majored in economics in college found Understanding by Design helpful, although she, too, said that "shaping a curriculum was difficult." She helped create a project called "money and rights," which looked at how wealth or lack of it affects a neighborhood. At a time when downtown Philadelphia was booming, learners discovered where money came from, why it was invested, how decisions were made, and what contributed to neighborhood revitalization. The project incorporated elements of math, social science, language arts, and science—the goal of all the projects. It culminated in learners creating business plans for the neighborhood, which were then critiqued by a group of fifteen community members.

Some of the other projects were driven by grants, such as one involving the Belmont Mansion, a site of the Underground Railroad. "We discussed slavery from the beginning of our nation through the Civil War and did a lot of study on the modern situation of African Americans," the educator said. Learners made full use of the Web, delved into primary sources, and made PowerPoint presentations rather than writing term papers and taking tests.

The year was divided into three segments, and learners moved from one project to another after a few months. Educators met in a huge group to plan final assessments after each learning cycle. The assessments, which rated learners on whether they were advanced, proficient, basic, below basic, or "not on the radar" (meaning they did little or no work), were narratives that gauged whether learners were meeting the competencies and gaining skills. There were no traditional grades or report cards.

Some of the older educators, especially, felt that this system didn't pay enough attention to the basic skills that many of these learners needed. "In the first year, if you ask[ed] me what curriculum I was using, I'd say, 'I don't know,'" said one educator, a career-changer who had been teaching for several years. If you asked educators to define project-based learning, "you'd probably get nine different answers."

One educator, a veteran of the Philadelphia system with certifications in English and history, prided herself on being a pioneer of creating service-based projects. She complained that "brand new educators that had never taught before and didn't know what had to be taught" were designing projects. "And yet," she said, "they had no idea what a project was."

On the one hand, this educator found the school district's core curriculum—imposed by Vallas at the same time he was encouraging multiple models of school design—to be stifling. At her prior school, she chafed at using literature anthologies (she preferred to have her students read novels like *Lord of the Flies*) and having to structure her lessons around separate reading groups—in which, she said, "the kids were never reading and the teacher was doing all the work."

At the same time, however, she argued that the core curriculum should be the reference point for learning at SOF. She felt that the projects devised primarily by her younger colleagues were insufficiently rigorous. "What I'm saying is I didn't really see a lot of content-driven materials," this educator said. "Yes, there are some nice projects, but when you look at the assessment of the students and what they have learned, show me concrete things that they've mastered."

According to almost everyone interviewed, this was a dilemma that plagued SOF. Microsoft's emphasis had always been on competencies, for both educators and learners, but the district's methods for measuring a school's progress depended on tests that assessed content knowledge. The conundrum of meshing the projects with the curricular demands of the school district was one of the points that divided the faculty. Some educators, mostly older, said that the inexperienced educators paid no attention to content. Others, mostly younger, argued that they were blazing new trails by emphasizing twenty-first-century skills instead of what they considered mile-wide, inch-deep survey courses.

IS IT MEASURABLE?

At the end of the first year, what the learners were actually learning was difficult to quantify, and certainly not immediately—a mortal sin in the current educational climate. The chief learner, some of the educators, and, to a large extent, Microsoft had initially thought that with the freedom to innovate they were given by Vallas, they would also be given time to show that their model could get more of these learners—so ill-served by traditional course structure and the four-year lockstep progression—ready for college and careers.

"Paul Vallas said we could be exempt from benchmarks [periodic testing], the core curriculum, any kind of standardized quantitative assessment," said one original faculty member. "He said it was OK to do projects instead of benchmarks, state-standards lesson plans instead of the core curriculum, primary source readings instead of textbooks. But . . . then he leaves and they say, 'This isn't transferable or transparent.' But it was never supposed to be." This educator said that she always assumed it would be important to make what SOF was doing "transferable and transparent" not to the school district's administrative machinery, but to college admissions officers. Higher education representatives who sat at the table at the conception of SOF "knew that the transcripts coming out of here would be different."

Many of the younger educators, who were the most devoted acolytes of the first chief learner, thought that the deliberately organic curriculum was working, in that it engaged the learners and brought out skills and talents that some didn't know they had. "The first year, kids who had not been successful at school achieved some success," said a young educator. "They were able to understand the world differently. They were exposed to different academic subjects in a way they hadn't been before. I believe that now they understand concepts rather than simply know[ing] them. The first year, we achieved that." Another said, "Some kids who are good test takers are challenged in ways [they're] not used to being challenged, such as presentation skills, taking action, exerting leadership . . . It was pretty successful, I thought."

To be sure, some learners at SOF thrived on the project model: for the first time, they finally connected to the point of school—to prepare them for jobs, for college, for a real work environment, for their futures. "It's different because it's project-based learning, that's a wonderful thing," said one learner during her third year. "It makes sense to me. When you go out into the world and get a job, it's not math here and history there but everything together. It's better to learn that way."

This young woman had had an undistinguished record in middle school and some discipline issues, which she said arose out of boredom. At SOF, she became a model learner. "It's also different, the feeling we get when we walk in here," she said. "In a regular school, the teacher is not giving you so much attention or time. But if I need help, a teacher could be walking out the door with her jacket on, but she'll take it off, sit down, and do work with me until six o'clock."

Others, used to worksheets, paper-and-pencil tests, and being asked to regurgitate information, simply found it bewildering. They were not used to taking control of their own education. One young woman who had attended a Catholic elementary school felt she wasn't learning anything unless she could amass multiple index cards. Doing everything on the computer was beyond her. She was among many who found it hard to adjust, and ultimately she transferred.

Even educators who saw major problems with the curriculum and other issues that first year said that the faculty members worked well together. "This was a happy place," said one veteran. Even so, different perspectives and disagreements manifested themselves virtually from the outset. Given the massive needs of the learners, divisions grew largely over whether to press ahead with the school's bold model or retreat to something more traditional.

CAN IT WORK?

Can this grand vision work for an inner-city, mostly African American population? Some educators, while eager for change and excited about the possibilities, ultimately concluded that the learners needed more academic structure, more stringent discipline, and more grounding in the basics. "They were coming out of one learning style, the orthodoxy of the system," said an older science educator who had come via the military and the business world. "They saw things as too separate, even though we were presenting it as unified. They couldn't comprehend this unity, coming from a prior way of being taught. There were two things, the change in pedagogy and the change in technology. They didn't have to go to a book and open it. The whole dynamic changed for them."

Educators were also divided by approaches to discipline. In the first year, the school tried a discipline policy that was an extension of the learning process, one that treated the learners as adults and gave them responsibility. It was a form of restorative justice, in which learners were asked to reflect on how their actions damaged the community and to give something back. It largely rejected the more punitive approach that relied on suspension, except for offenses that involved fighting or violence.

For some of the younger educators, this made perfect sense. "We were asking kids to . . . be project managers, recorders, artists, create teams," said one educator. Instead of multiple suspensions, "punishment" often consisted of discussion, reading, and service. One tactic the original chief learner used was to deprive the learners temporarily of their laptops and make them read a book that would force them to reflect on their transgression. However, somehow the word got out that learners were trashing their laptops (that first year, thirty-seven were damaged, destroyed, or lost) and that the school was not under control. To be sure, this young educator said, some learners took advantage of the loose scheduling. "There was real teenage testing the limits," she said. "And I think because the limits were so vast at that point, there was a lot of testing that went on. [But] this was not a scary place. This was not a violent place."

Other educators—and again, they were mostly older—complained that the lack of structure, rules, and systems was ill-suited to the learners in the building. Some went so far as to suggest that for all its emphasis on competencies in assembling the educator team, Microsoft had not paid enough attention to one: so-called cultural competency, or the ability to relate to learners from different backgrounds. Even though the competencies included valuing diversity, one African American educator said that the first chief learner, who was white, once asked him if she needed to go back to school to learn how to teach African American students. He said no, that it was more a matter of better understanding where they were coming from.

While each educator had complex and even internally contradictory views on what the learners needed, for the most part the divisions tended to divide along age and, to some extent, racial lines. Generally, though, they divided along the lines of experience.

"There's traditional thinking and untraditional thinking," said one first-year hire, who was an experienced Philadelphia teacher. "It's not that [the older educators would] rather teach out of textbook [than use technology]." It was that they were sometimes frustrated by "overzealous actions" they felt were a product of inexperience. "They feel offended [that] young ones are making changes [and they are thinking,] 'How are you making changes, what proof do you have that's going to work? I know this won't work, why do that, why don't you ask one who had done it?'"

The original chief learner lasted long enough into that first summer to hire the second cohort of educators. This time, among the eight brought on to teach core subjects, six were brand new, three of them from the University of Pennsylvania's accelerated alternative certification graduate program. Two were district veterans, one a science teacher with twenty-four years in the district, primarily at a middle school. In that first tumultuous summer, the first group set out to train the second. The woman who was eventually appointed the chief learner in 2008, who during that summer worked in the Office of Secondary Education at district headquarters, was brought in to help the educators plan for the second year.

It was a difficult time.

"They were all gung-ho to show us, but they also were heartbroken [at the loss of the chief learner]," one second-year hire said of the first group. "And they were, like, 'This is what we do here.' But nobody could tell us what Tuesday at 11 a.m. looks like. They could tell us, 'This is what a final project that we did last year looked like.' But there was no sense of what happened to create that final project in our training." Another second-year hire said the two cohorts of educators had "digital contact through e-mail" and other computer-based means. While that was "more interaction than would happen in most places," she said that it was not until August first that the two cohorts met together for a big orientation. "It was, 'This is, like, where we are. And these are the struggles we're going to have.'"

There was team-building that August, said this educator, "but there was tension because we came into a place that wasn't what we signed up for. We signed up to have a leader and pursue something. And all of a sudden, no leader, no discipline, no nothing, it seemed, for us. So there was a tension between the two groups." Explicit technology training was more technical than philosophical, and broad based.

In the leadership vacuum, a group of educators from both groups got together to rethink and rewrite the curriculum—they were, after all, hired in part because of their leadership and problem-solving competencies. They were supported and largely left alone by the interim chief learner, who had been sent in the fall to hold down the fort until a new permanent chief learner could be found.

"We started to differentiate instruction, we started to put into place a model for advancement," said one educator. Specifically, the curriculum writers developed project levels—100, 200, 300, and 400—much how courses in college are ranked for difficulty. The unifying question of inquiry was, "Who am I?" around issues of borders and identity. An outside consultant was brought in by Microsoft to help the educator scaffold the projects—how to take the learners from step one to step two to step three, and how to align the skills used in the projects with the state standards.

Learners were individually evaluated to see what level of project they could handle, and they were assigned to projects based on how much they had achieved, not how long they had been in the school. Some second- and third-year learners who were way behind wound up in level-one projects, while level four was for advanced learners. "[With] the project model we created, which is basically an accelerated model, learners advance at their own pace," explained one educator instrumental in its creation. "They can graduate early, stay later. There's no social promotion. And it's based off of the skills they learn, not the content that they have to take. And those skills are the competencies . . . They had to achieve proficiency in those competencies before moving up to the next level. That idea was very novel in a high school."

But one educator said she felt lost. While she had chafed at restrictions at her prior school and was looking for a freer rein, she lost her bearings for a time at SOF. "It was like being in a huge meadow and in every direction were blades of grass, and you are told to pick one," she said. "I'm a problem-solver and a hard worker, but I like to know my parameters. I didn't have a parameter, and I didn't know how to solve problems."

Many educators were invested in the new curriculum and felt it was working, although its implementation varied depending on the particular groups. But the year, with the roiling leadership, was chaotic. Learner discipline began to deteriorate. The divisions among the faculty became more acute.

A new chief learner, intended at the time to be permanent, came in December of that second year. She had run a successful elementary school but had no high school experience. At SOF, she wanted to retain projects and understood that the school was created to do things differently. By inclination, though, she preferred more traditional systems and wondered about the new instructional model's ability to produce the kinds of test scores and results the district was looking for. In admitting the next class of learners, she briefly flirted with trying to screen students for admission rather than choosing them by lottery—an approach that had been rejected by the school's designers, including Microsoft. Even after the bumpy start, Microsoft and their allies in Philadelphia were still determined to find a replicable model for the typical inner-city neighborhood high school.

But after the school's second year, the second chief learner was gone as well, promoted by the new superintendent to lead one of the district's regions. The school was leaderless again, and to fill the void, the new superintendent, Arlene Ackerman, sent to the school as chief learner a well-respected district veteran who had been principal of a science-oriented magnet high school and worked in the secondary education office. As such, she had participated in the school's start-up planning and had helped the first two faculty cohorts get through the previous summer. "I almost felt obligated to come," this woman said. "I was at the table when we talked about 'what if.'" She came into an atmosphere of turmoil and uncertainty, with pressure for measurable results growing from "downtown."

Through the end of the second year and the beginning of the third, educators at SOF were still using the staff-developed curriculum, teaching through projects and working in teams. But the new leader's mandate, as she candidly acknowledges, was to make what was happening at SOF transparent and transferable to the central office. That meant, for the most part, adopting the district's core curriculum, creating one-subject classes and a more traditional schedule, and covering content that could be tested on weekly exams that were now being required for neighborhood high schools. This was also the first year that SOF learners, the eleventh graders, would be taking Pennsylvania's state standardized tests, so there was pressure for conventional test prep.

In the fall, the new chief learner called a retreat of a small group of educators to rethink the instructional program. The team was left with little choice but to adopt the district's scheduling and core curriculum the following February, reverting to subject-matter courses, with two short periods in the middle of the day reserved for projects. Some of the educators, primarily the younger ones and those who had worked in that second fall to develop the curriculum, were devastated and embittered. They felt that acceding to the district's demands for more structure and more standard content amounted to abandoning the vision of the school and its theory of change. They felt that this decision obliterated all their work.

However flawed it may have been, said one frustrated young educator who was in the vanguard of the curriculum development, "We came up with it. We came up with a system. It was something that we developed as educators." He decried the unwillingness of some of his colleagues to do serious rethinking of the educational model, something that he had done even before being hired by the first chief learner, whom he called regularly before he had even finished his master's program. "The fault line is [that] people here need to ask fundamental questions," this educator said. "Not everybody asks fundamental questions. They want to teach the way they've been teaching at their traditional high schools. They want the kids to learn the way they learned when they were in high school. And they don't want to ask questions about their content areas that are fundamental, like, should everybody learn about Shakespeare?" Before the order to begin using the core curriculum, he was helping a team of girls understand math and physics by designing a complicated double-dutch jump-rope game. Afterward, when his course morphed into Algebra I, he was drawing number lines on the whiteboard (albeit using Microsoft OneNote to manipulate the graphs).

Other educators, however, were either conflicted, indifferent, or in favor of the change. "On some days, I think it is not the worst thing in the world and it actually could be helpful," said one of the first-year educators about making more use of the core curriculum. "On others, I think it is the worst thing I ever heard." She had invested a lot of time teaching mostly geometry to 100-level learners by having them study how different countries use resources compared to their area and population. "We looked at which countries were more selfish or less, using volume, area, shapes, and so forth." The 200-level project was more algebra heavy, as the core curriculum called for algebra before geometry. "I think there are better ways to [address gaps in knowledge] than the core curriculum," this educator said. She understood how it "gives new educators a place to start." But, she added, "instead of innovating properly, we're grasping for straws. That's the worst thing."

One of the two experienced educators hired in the second year, who had spent most of her two decades in the district at a difficult middle school, had a completely different perspective. "I'm fine with that, I'm an easy person," she said of the decision to adopt the core curriculum. "Whatever the district says . . . I'll do what needs to be done."

This educator was happy enough to teach using projects, collaborate with colleagues, learn new things, and was thrilled after decades at a troubled middle school to be at a place like SOF, which, for all the discipline issues that flared in the troubled second year, seemed to her like Nirvana. Instinctually, she realized that she had to build some of her teaching around her learners' interests and thought projects were a good way to do that. She admired the energy of her young colleagues, "even though most of them are young enough to be my children."

Another older science educator, however, said that the projects often put the cart before the horse:

> You can't talk about heart failure and disease without going into basic cell function. There are too many gaps, and the kids being young and underdeveloped can't see the connection. They don't see how [it] all fits together and interlinks. They miss the continuity of understanding. Now you have a kid who could have done great on a project, but if you give him a standardized test for content, [he] would do terribly.

For the fourth school year, a faculty committee called Curriculum 2010 is at work redesigning the curriculum to meld the best aspects of project-based and interdisciplinary learning with the school district's core curriculum and state standards.

TECHNOLOGY

Although grounded in technology, SOF has never had a formal technology coordinator or taught the learners how to be "techies." Nor has it screened educators for their particular comfort with technology, other than using an online application process. Instead, it was expected that technology would be embedded throughout the school, the driving force for everything it did. While learners were trained how to use their computers, which included tablet and regular laptops, SOF has not offered courses like "introduction to computing" or programming.

The most commonly used software is Microsoft OneNote, which makes it much easier for learners to organize notes and embed drawings, and it automatically includes citations when something is cut and pasted from the Web. Textbooks can be downloaded right into the program. It can include not just hyperlinks and pictures, but audio and video files. This facilitates projects—a class doing a project on world nutrition, for instance, can easily include videos and create mini-books.

While educators received some training in OneNote, they all use it differently; some are much more likely to take full advantage of it than others. If you ask educators how they view and use technology in general, the answers will vary widely, from being utterly transformative to just another tool in the toolbox. All educators use it for communication and assignments, because there are no textbooks and technically no paper. One educator confessed to never having learned how to operate a Promethean board, much less something more complicated.

Some educators were content for learners to use their laptops as fancy notebooks. "I view [technology] as a facilitator," said a science educator, who was hired in the school's third year. "And that's even part of our mission . . . it's a facilitator of learning. It's not a crutch, or it's not the rock I put my teaching on. I use this as a tool, just like a calculator. I do all of it. I use the projector. They're all tools."

This educator grew up in a rough small city outside Philadelphia and traveled the educational gauntlet himself. He barely graduated from high school and flunked out of community college. He made his way to SOF via the Marine Corps, Iraq, and Penn State, where he earned two degrees, a BA in history and a BS in biology. His wife turned him on to the Philadelphia Teaching Fellows program, an alternative certification program for college graduates. He spent several months in a problem-ridden middle school—where, he said, he had forty-year-old history books. When that school was first turned over to a private provider and then simply earmarked for closing, he found SOF at a site-selection job fair.

Given his own background, this educator sees technology primarily as a tool to build relationships with learners. He warned that educators must be careful not to use it to create distance. "The primary learning is a one-to-one, me and the learner . . . and how I connect to them and how I break down those barriers of mistrust," he said. He noted that education has failed many of them and they still feel "mistrust of the teacher, mistrust of the administration, mistrust of the school district."

For another educator, who has a degree in the subject, technology is all-encompassing. It profoundly affects the way young people comprehend and process information—they prefer to focus on pictures, music, and sound. They have learned to have multiple identities—one for MySpace, one for IM—each representing a different mode of how they interact, all of which all has implications for pedagogy and curriculum. Even so, this educator said, "they come with zero technological skills," little beyond knowing how to instant message and find a Web page.

This educator talked about "old ways to do old things" (the transmission of information from teacher and textbook to student), "new ways to do old things" (digital notebooks), and "new ways to do new things" (Wikis, virtual classrooms that tie students to others around the world). "I like to think about this school as a global mode of education that should be enhancing the experience of the kids," he said, adding that he was frustrated that the full promise of the school was not yet being realized.

Most of the educators, regardless of whether they were in the vanguard or are bringing up the rear on the issue of technology, agreed on one thing: they felt that they should have control over the learners' laptops. Microsoft, however, had a reason not to make the software to do that available immediately: the idea that "IMing" and playing games were just newfangled ways of passing notes to a friend and looking out the window instead of paying attention. Those who conceived the school felt that educators should have the tools to keep the learners engaged, rather than relying on crutches (like controlling learners' computers) to limit distractions.

But it seems that virtually none of the educators were convinced of that. "I would spend thirty to sixty minutes of a period deleting games from the computer," lamented one educator. "Students would be instant messaging and checking e-mails during class. When you're exhausted because you've been telling kids to stop playing Halo all day, you're not actually teaching them literature or skills or the content that they need to drive their own learning."

Another issue that arose when the decision was made to adopt the core curriculum is that the school had no budget to buy textbooks. Most of the district's texts and written materials were also available online or in CD or DVD versions, but figuring out where to get traditional materials and how to use them became a problem.

Discovering when he arrived on the first day of school in 2008 that nobody knew he had been hired was not the only shock facing the out-of-state Spanish teacher. He had no materials or curriculum to work with. And no direction, since this was the first time foreign language educators had been hired. There had been no advance planning for how to integrate them into the projects. This time he was rescued by his mother, who works for a Delaware school district that was adopting a new Spanish textbook series and offered him the old ones. The chief learner initially said no to this offer because "they wanted to keep SOF textbook free," but he cajoled her into agreeing.

So, with the books donated by his mom, he and the other Spanish educator were able to offer two classes. "It's not very futuristic, having to scrounge around," he laughed. "Luckily, my own education is rooted in the past, and luckily, I've taught before. However, I was taken aback, to say the least." He said that he is planning how to use technology to teach Spanish. "Students can write letters to the editor of a newspaper in another country," he said. "I can mail-merge the letters and see exactly when each student sent it." But, more than that, the potential exists for SOF learners to interact with students in Spanish-speaking countries remotely, while each sits in their own classroom. "I do think this is a school of the future because of the way the technology has been integrated," he said.

CONCLUSION

There is agreement among faculty members that SOF can't just become like any other neighborhood school—that is not its mission or purpose. Beyond that, views and approaches diverge. The school district, with entirely new leadership than the group that instigated SOF's founding, is concerned about making what happens there transparent and transferable so it can be evaluated using state and district assessments, but it also recognizes the school's uniqueness.

There is still a question of whether the full power of the new technology is being tapped by the school's instructional program. Laptops, for example, have proven to be both a boon and a distraction. Whether the school can fully use its technology depends on the technology of the district as a whole. Districts as large as Philadelphia, especially in this high-stakes era, are built on conformity in curriculum and assessments. Its computerized methods for assessing student progress and evaluating schools couldn't handle what SOF was giving them—for example, narrative report cards instead of familiar letter grades. Additionally, learners may have completed a terrific project in the neighborhood based on the Census, but questions arose to whether they had taken algebra and if so, if they passed it. Moreover, with the people who helped conceive and create the school gone, the district leadership has been unwilling to wait and see how many SOF learners are able to graduate or get into and succeed in college as an indicator of the school's success.

The hiring process carefully honed by Microsoft yielded far more brand new and young educators than older, experienced ones, but it was compromised by other concerns—the district's cumbersome hiring process that forced some last-minute decisions, multiple changes in leadership, shifting views of what the school needed. "We're being forced to do these things because of consistency," said one educator. It comes from a view of education that "we need to be consistent about everything that we do, which is translated into, we need to do the same thing everywhere. And if we need to do the same thing everywhere, how can we have one school that gets this privilege of doing whatever they want?"

This constant tug-of-war occurs at all levels. At the same time the central office is requiring SOF to adapt its curriculum and systems to the rest of the system, it is also suggesting high school reform measures in a five-year strategic plan that mirror some of what the school has been attempting: flexible schedules, more project-based learning, more time for educators to work in teams, to name a few.[8] And district officials are taking a new look at the school to see both what the district can learn from it and how it can be improved. Nevertheless, three years after it opened, the school is at a crossroads. Despite all it has attempted, it will, like all other neighborhood schools, be judged by whether its learners do well on state standardized tests.

Educators, even those who would consider themselves traditional, know that losing the edge of innovation would be a mistake. They are trying to be optimistic. "The school is still intact to do education in a different and pioneering way," said an older educator. "I just don't think we're there yet to transition the human element," meaning a student body that lacks skills and motivation and is easily frustrated. "We haven't sat down and really considered the technology aspects along with the academic element that's before us," this educator said.

But the commitment was to create a school that would figure out how to address the needs of those very learners. One educator asked, "If we're just going to become another comprehensive high school, how are we the School of the Future?"

Recommendations

At School of the Future, the pendulum has swung from the original chief learners' completely organic vision to the more rigid model of a core curriculum in which learners are evaluated primarily by periodic paper-and-pencil testing. What is needed is a melding of the two—a clearer understanding at SOF of what is meant by rigor and standards, while they still find ways to be interdisciplinary and project based. The school district's strategic plan is broad enough for SOF to be the prime testing ground for some of its initiatives, including new models for a comprehensive, nonselective high school. The school and the district should work together to make it happen.

Professional communities develop when there is a regular time and place set aside for shared conversation about student learning. Educator teams at SOF have already set a precedent for meeting and holding regular discussions of what is working and what is not. These gatherings need to be embedded in the school day, and the school must establish some structured routines to make that possible.

While SOF has paid more attention to professional development than most schools, there seems to be a need for a greater focus on explicit technology training for its educators and to develop a common understanding of its potential. The district should also look at its own technological capacity in order to understand and evaluate what is going on at a school like School of the Future in terms of schedules and courses completed by students.

The curriculum developed during the school's second year could be a starting point for SOF to achieve the goal in the district's strategic plan to build a more relevant and engaging high school curriculum. The school can also work to refine that curriculum and develop projects that do not have to be reimagined every year, and which can be adapted to changing circumstances and particular learner interests and skills while still meeting content standards and making full use of the school's technology.

States and school districts have to figure out what they really want, innovation or conformity. This is true in evaluating charter schools or a school like SOF, which was created to break the mold. School of the Future, with its forward-looking, technology-based innovations, is playing out the debate over whether or not the structure of schooling can change dramatically—especially for underserved urban students who are clearly not making it in the traditional structures. Students in Philadelphia and elsewhere would be well served if the district and community supported efforts to fulfill its original vision.

7

When the Model Works

Snapshots from the Classrooms

Kate Hayes, Deleah Archer-Neal, Kate Reber, Thomas Emerson,
Thomas Gaffey, and Aruna Arjunan

NO ONE EVER TOLD us this would be easy. And it isn't. Creating school structures and systems, redefining culture, writing project-based curriculum, maintaining partnerships, preparing for the PSSA, PSAT, ACT, SAT—all of this is daunting and overwhelming. Yet, it is also tremendously exciting for us as educators, who signed on with School of the Future because we truly believe that high school can and must look different for the children and families of West Philadelphia, and for our country at large.

You could characterize us as idealists, workaholics, perfectionists, foster moms and dads, reformists, debaters, academics, and lifelong learners. We are the ones in the ring each day, working to create a better way for our learners to learn. Some of us have been with this project since it started and some have joined along the way, but each of us has been engaged passionately in the creation of SOF.

There have been many iterations of our program and of teaching and learning at SOF—some more traditional, others more learner driven and deeply constructivist in nature. But all of the learning has been deliberate and aligned with the Pennsylvania State Standards. As professionals entrusted with the lives and education of future citizens, we take on each teaching and learning opportunity with a fervent commitment to excellence, rigor, and the personal learning and development of our learners and ourselves.

What we look for in our learners is unique. Test scores are important, but hardly enough. When a learner walks out of our doors for the last time, we want to ensure that he or she is ready to engage twenty-first-century society in a meaningful way. To this end, we strive to create an environment that is continuous, relevant, and adaptive, one where all learners are engaged in hands-on learning that promotes inquisitiveness, leadership, teamwork, and personal growth. We assess our learners' education competencies—a collection of characteristics, attributes, behaviors, and skills found in successful learners, educators, and professionals—alongside traditional assessment of core curriculum content. Twelve education competencies were specially selected by a planning committee for the SOF learners, educators, and administrators, drawing on Microsoft's existing system for professional development. These skills add a real-world dimension to our learning and model of assessment, which requires our learners to work toward proficiency when working alone or in teams, presenting information, problem-solving, and managing relationships. We hold all learners and educators responsible for their personal development of these competencies as part of learning and working at SOF.

We face large challenges: fourteen- to sixteen-year-old learners with fourth-grade reading levels and years of below-basic test scores; families with significant economic, social, and personal hardships that make it almost impossible for our learners to focus consistently on learning; and extensive leadership turnover that has left many of us grasping for direction and assurance that the innovative project we began three years ago will continue. But if we only focus on these issues, you will never hear the story about our first school musical, *Dreamgirls*, or how one learner successfully facilitated her own class. You won't understand the role that we strive to play in our learners' lives as advisors, project mentors, and guides for just-in-time learning. You will never hear about a performance of understanding (POU) or how our learners advocated for and made presentations on community issues and needs relevant to them.

What follows are vignettes that depict cases where educators and learners have succeeded in developing competencies beyond the traditional measures. Although you will find examples of many different skills and attributes within each story, the competencies specifically highlighted are featured in the title of each vignette. It is our hope that these stories will give shape and perspective to the successes experienced by learners and educators at SOF.

MANAGERIAL COURAGE AND VALUING DIVERSITY

What if a learner could design and teach her own class to address a need she has identified in her community and promote the development of competencies in her peers? This was the daunting question faced by an SOF learner, Q, and me, her "counseling educator," during an independent research project.

When I took the job of counseling educator, one thing was made perfectly clear—I was not to be a traditional school counselor. Thankful for my days as a substitute teacher and prior work in service learning, I was quickly thrust into the role of educator with classes of my own to design and facilitate. The skills I was to cover were our twelve SOF learner competencies, which included creativity, managing relationships, and decision quality and problem solving. So, as I embarked on my own learning and development path, exercising my competency in dealing with ambiguity and learning on the fly, I watched my learners do the same. Whether we were designing a mentorship program, organizing parent night, or hosting a community art exhibit and dinner, our collective challenges in project management, leadership, diversity of opinion, and integrity resulted in many lessons learned. Some lessons came through difficult mistakes, when our grand ideals met head-on with reality, and many of our incremental yet meaningful successes came when learners collaborated to enhance their community and work as a team.

One particular success evolved as Q, now seventeen years old and a fourth-year learner, embraced learner-driven projects and the culture of SOF. Q was not always connected to the process of learning: her middle school records show a mixture of successes and areas needing improvement. At times she was a fighter, an absentee, and disengaged from her classes and peers, all of which prevented her from going to one of the special admission schools in Philadelphia and ultimately landed her at SOF in her neighborhood of West Philly. It was within the unique SOF learner leadership opportunities that Q started to find her passion for advocacy and education.

In 2007, SOF began its program for learners with autism. We welcomed our new learners into the community with the philosophy of mainstreaming, or integrating, these learners into our projects, classrooms, and community as much as possible. At first this proved overwhelming and largely unsuccessful. The classroom communities did not embrace the learners with autism as we had hoped; rather, they teased them and feared their presence. Unbeknownst to the typical SOF learners, they had always been in classes with learners of different abilities. In fact, all of our learners with specific learning disabilities (SLD) were mainstreamed and team taught, rather than pulled out for special classes. Our SLD learners had enjoyed a sense of anonymity and inclusion, yet the eccentricities of autism proved too visible for this same seamless integration without a specific and targeted education plan. In our racially and economically homogeneous environment, we found ourselves faced with our first test for developing the competency of valuing diversity in our learners and staff. A second-year learner rose to this challenge.

Q witnessed the unsuccessful mainstreaming of her autistic peers and resented the intolerance she saw in her classrooms. "This shouldn't be that hard!" she would comment to her educators and mentors throughout the school. "Can I help make it better?" As an educator, this question was music to my ears. Knowing that we needed to attack this issue with clear and consistent messages to our learners, and that any message would be exponentially more effective if it came from a peer, Q was the perfect leader to take on the challenge. "Write a proposal, Q!" was my response. Here is an excerpt from Q's reflections on her brainstorming process, followed by a quote from her proposal letter:

Ms. Hayes, the school counselor, and I came up with a brilliant idea! We have mini projects at school two days a week for an hour and a half each day. Well she thought it would be great if I worked with the learners with autism during this time. I loved the idea more than anything at this point. She also informed me that I would have to write a proposal. "A proposal?!" is what was going through my head at the time. I knew what a proposal was, I just never saw [or wrote] one prior to this conversation. I knew I had to do some research. My mother is ALWAYS the first step to my research. I asked my mom and she said a good proposal took time and a lot of effort. She also told me she had never had to do one, however she did help a friend while they were in college. My mom gave me some ideas . . . I then looked up some things on MSN. My last research stop [for the proposal] was Ms. Robin. This lady knew just what to say . . . It sounded to me like I had my work cut out for me.

I don't believe that children with autism in public schools are graduating with the life skills they need to succeed in life. I also pretty much dislike what I see in our school towards the children with autism. I believe that children with autism have a lot to offer to us if we show them how. I feel like someone needs to step up to the plate and give them what they deserve. School shouldn't be a daycare for them; it should be a great learning experience.[1]

After a PowerPoint presentation to the chief learner and special education liaison, the first phase of Q's independent study was granted. Together, Q and I investigated the deep need we saw within the SOF community—to transform schoolwide behaviors and attitudes toward learners with autism. Given the relevant and adaptive nature of SOF's educational program, Q was able to pose her own questions and use the technology and community members' personal connections to research the answers. After six months of learner-driven research, interviews, and observations, Q's conclusion was to create and teach her own mini-project for her peers. Another proposal and presentation was needed, and she received support from the school community, partners, and administration. The following is an excerpt from that proposal:

At School of the Future, learners have an opportunity to design their own projects. The class that I [want to] create is called All In Together. This class is constructed to help build life skills for learners with autism, as well as a buddy program for all interested learners in our school. The class is also a way to help us learn to accept differences and disabilities. Our class [will be] open and welcome to whomever is willing to be open minded and ready to learn. This learning cycle, we will touch on social skills, speaking, presenting and cooking skills, just to name a few. While we will have a lot of fun, we still are sure to stay on top of our work, be [responsible] for our actions and respectful at all times! At the beginning of each class, I have planned a "Do Now" [an activity to get the class warmed up] and an Ice Breaker. Our "Do Now's" are questions to answer or quotes for the learners to respond to. Our Ice Breakers are fun team building activities that get us in the mood to learn and do work![2]

Q and I wrote a syllabus for our class, which outlined our scope and sequence. Q was to be the facilitator and I the guide on the side, stepping in when needed. When mini-project selection time began in February, All In Together was listed as a choice. Many learners selected the project and a screening process proved necessary. We only needed ten learners to buddy with our seven autistic learners and two learners with traumatic brain injuries. Q held interviews, selected her team of buddies, distributed the syllabus, and embarked on her own project design. The goal was to spend a few weeks together as a class, working on buddy relationships, social skills, and advocacy language. One day a week we would take some time with just the buddies to address concerns and have conversations about their process. After about four weeks, we hoped to have the buddy pairs select a second mini-project that they would attend together for one of the two days. The buddies would be able to help the learners with autism slowly assimilate into the class. They would also be available to teach their peers about autism and promote the competency of valuing diversity in the classroom. The following is Q's reflection on making her vision a reality:

THINGS DID NOT GO AS PLANNED! The first few classes were pleasant. We listed things that we really wanted to be able to do. These were things that we couldn't [make happen] because . . . maybe we just let the putdowns that were thrown at us [by our peers] get the best of us. We started a letter to these people . . . [The buddies] enjoyed [the class at first] because I was there along the way telling them that they could indeed do it. I felt like a proud mother and they were happy. The sixth day of class was unpleasant to the learners [when they] were told that we would have to pick another class for these learners to go to and I would be able to visit their classes. They were all a little afraid because the classes . . . were with the regular population of the school. My first thought was just "OMG!" I wasn't too sure about it; however, I'm still a learner so I had to [try it]. We did it. Weeks went by . . . I think all but three of us were unhappy and sad. Would things get better?[3]

At SOF, we believe that learning comes through failing and then adjusting for success. Our plan was not working as we hoped. The learners with autism were still experiencing teasing in the second project and the buddies, who had formed personal relationships and bonds with their learners, were upset to witness this intolerant behavior and found themselves unable to advocate for their buddies in a strong and effective way. We needed to regroup, fortify our structures, and rejuvenate our team. Q's reflection follows:

I talked to Ms. Hayes and told her this wasn't working out for us. [She said,] "No one ever said this way was the right way. So we need to try something new!" Those were the only words I needed to hear. That's when things took a turn for the better. Ms. Hayes and I did research, read to one another, and looked at videos to see what would be a good way to handle the problem at hand. We found some interesting and fun things.[4]

Q and I enlisted the help of our staff and community connections. We arranged more in-depth training for our buddies with experts in the fields of education, service learning, and autism from local universities, agencies, and schools. We redefined the expectations for our buddies: their goal was no longer to feel the stress of participating in two different projects, but to concentrate on helping their learners with autism accomplish their social goals inside the second project. We solicited feedback from the educators of the second projects and allowed more time for group reflection about the process and experience of mainstreaming. Finally, we focused our collective final project on education for the rest of the school to help create more acceptance and awareness of difference.

When we held our concluding class that spring, it was evident that Q's project successfully transformed the hearts and minds of her peers about autism. Learners gushed about their experiences and the feeling of taking on a challenge together, valuing diversity, and being action oriented—three key SOF competencies. Additionally, Q accomplished another goal that was not anticipated: she sparked a schoolwide interest in independent projects.

Q will continue with this as her senior project in her fourth year, which is required to graduate from high school in Pennsylvania and from SOF. Other learners have also begun their own senior projects, addressing different needs that they see in their community. It is our hope as educators that the skills and competencies gained through this type of project-based, action-oriented learning will assist in the development of twenty-first-century learners and citizens.

MANAGING RELATIONSHIPS AND MANAGING PROCESSES AND SYSTEMS

In many schools around the nation, you will find a period in the day called advisory. This period often is used simply to record attendance and distribute schoolwide newsletters and other school documents. The length of the period varies from school to school, as does the function. However, at SOF, we have a different approach to advisory.

Advisory is one of the strategies we use to personalize education. Each learner is assigned to an educator, who becomes an advocate and supporter for the learner. By creating these personal connections, students can begin to feel safe and supported and, as research shows, do better in school. During our first and second year, advisory met once a day for approximately forty-five minutes. This time was devoted to building relationships among advisory members and reinforcing basic skills using online reading, writing, and math programs. Learners are assigned to advisories by incoming year, and an effort is made to separate learners who come from the same middle schools or neighborhoods, thus giving learners the chance to meet new peers. As they move through their high school years, they continue with the same advisory. Both educators and learners develop a bond and identity that is unique to their group.

To help foster relationships across classes, or years, we developed a system to connect the advisories that embodies our global approach to education. In our first year of advisories, each group adopted the name of one of the continents. Each new advisory group in the second year chose a country from within each continent and became a brother or sister advisory to a continent advisory. Our next incoming group chose a city within one of the countries. And, in 2009–2010, our last group chose animal species from within one of the countries. At the end of our first four years, we will begin the cycle of naming the advisories again.

As a fourth-year educator, I've had the pleasure of working with the Asia Advisory. Originally I was not assigned to this group, but we lost the Asia advisor shortly after school opened. Each advisor had a back-up to provide assistance when needed, and as Asia's back-up, I assumed the role. Over the years, I've grown to love my kids and develop a strong connection with them. They in turn have affectionately adopted me as a foster mom.

During the 2007–2008 school year, in addition to guiding our learners through the Web-based education programs Rosetta Stone, Apex, and Criterion, we were charged with creating a team project during advisory. As we looked around our classroom, which had dozens of bookcases and shelves, we decided there was no better way to use this space than to create a College Resource Center. To help organize this project, we developed a weekly schedule. Each day, we used advisory time to accomplish a specific task. On Fridays we worked on our College Resource Center project.

So, we had the vision—we were going to create a resource center. Why? Well, many of my learners knew they wanted to go to college, but they knew little about the college admissions process or even what options were available to them. They had many questions, and they wanted a resource center that could guide them down the right path. They wanted information, and lots of it. I know you might be thinking, "They have computers and the Internet. There's a wealth of information just waiting for them!" And you are correct. However, the learners wanted tangible evidence. They wanted a room where they could sit and browse through a college or university brochure. They wanted information devoted to a major or area of interest to them and lists of scholarship opportunities. Most important, they wanted to design a physical space that would cater to their postsecondary needs.

We needed materials and we wanted to decorate the resource center with college and university paraphernalia. Divide and conquer was our plan. First, we created a request letter template. This letter asked for brochures, applications, scholarship information, financial aid information, and donations of paraphernalia. Then we divided up the task of e-mailing the letter to colleges and universities, enlisting the help of the other continent and country advisories. Our advisory took on the challenge of e-mailing the majority of colleges and universities in the United States.

The first day of sending letters was interesting. I didn't micromanage this venture because I wanted the learners to navigate and find their way. In doing so, they were working on their ability to learn on the fly. Many learners didn't know where to find the admissions contact on a college Web site. Some received responses from admissions personnel with a link to an application portal. At times it was frustrating and they wanted to give up. I would hear, "Did they not read the letter? We said mail it, not e-mail it!" However, once the materials began to arrive, the project became a competition of who could get the most mailings in a week. Every Friday, I passed out the mailings, calling them by state. The learners were so excited when they heard their state called—they couldn't wait to see what was sent. And if the college or university sent some paraphernalia, you would have thought they had hit the jackpot! We learned a lot through the College Resource Center project: the learners worked to manage relationships among themselves, the other continents, and college and university professionals. We became a team, and we celebrated our successes and our ability to create something for SOF that learners needed.

As I reflect on this project, I see that it helped our learners develop another competency, strategic agility and innovation management. Microsoft defines this competency as being able to "[anticipate] future consequences and trends accurately; [bring] creative ideas to market; [recognize] strategic opportunities for change; [create] competitive and breakthrough strategies."[5] My learners understood that in order to reach their goal of attaining a college education, they needed a place where they could focus on that goal.

Collecting college materials was the first step in creating a college-going culture at SOF. We have had several other efforts to help further this process. Our partners at Villanova helped make the physical space of the resource center a reality. A group of service-learning students from Villanova teamed up with learners and the counseling educator at SOF to design a space that would house all of our college materials, as well as test-prep books, college and career guides, and many other resources needed for the higher education admissions process. The Villanova students raised funds to purchase comfortable furniture, lighting, shelving, and artwork for the room. In 2008–2009, we also created a mini-project for rising senior learners called Career and College Awareness. In this class, some of the connections made through requesting materials for the resource center were tapped again, this time as speakers. As we look forward to our first round of college applications in 2009–2010, we know that the College Resource Center and the connections and relationships fostered with universities and colleges will prove invaluable. The project remains a work in progress and is constantly growing to support the learners and a college-going culture at SOF.

ACTION ORIENTED, AND PERSONAL LEARNING AND DEVELOPMENT

As educators at School of the Future, we are asked to draw on many things in our classroom teaching. We are given numerous technological tools. At times we balance conflicting curricular demands—multiple subject areas, School District of Philadelphia core curricula, and a project-based humanities curriculum that we began to develop in the spring of 2008. We also must keep in mind the learning competencies, the success factors and key attributes found in successful learners, which we sometimes assess or incorporate in our projects but rarely explicitly teach. At times I find it challenging to integrate distinct content areas, skill sets, and learning competencies in my lessons and projects. At other times, it is especially clear to me that integration and competency-based instruction enhances learning. The unit I planned on current issues in constitutional law was one of my more successful attempts at teaching with and toward learning competencies.

The unit itself, and particularly the culminating demonstration of learning called a performance of understanding, created opportunities for learners to build competency as action-oriented decision makers, and in terms of their own personal learning and development. A POU is more than just jargon. Instead of a dressed-up final project, this mode of assessment puts learners in a position where they must construct new understanding in the development of a final product. As was often the case with the learning competencies, I did not explicitly teach or directly assess the competencies in this particular unit. I find this regrettable and frustrating, because I feel that competencies can be well used when they are an intentional part of our curriculum and instruction. Still, I think the competencies play an interesting role in the discussion of this unit and its successes and failures because they are almost a naturally occurring part of the education process. Even without my intending to incorporate these skills in my lesson plans, they emerged and strengthened the learning experience.

The Current Constitutional Issues unit was part of an American history and English course for third-year learners, taught in a double-weighted, single-period course. The learners in this class saw me five times a week, for three forty-seven-minute and two sixty-seven-minute periods, and they received credit for both American history and English. The class began in February and ended in June, so we had one semester to cover a great deal of material. The first unit focused on ideas of the American dream and poetry. We then read *Lord of the Flies,* examining political philosophies and theories of governance as they connected to the novel and to the American Revolution. This unit on the Constitution came in the middle of the semester, right after spring break.

The unit began with an investigation of the U.S. Constitution, framed by a discussion of rights and responsibilities. To ground our studies in the document itself, learners had to investigate the structure of the articles and amendments so they would know where to look for answers when they did their own research. The introductory piece of the unit also included a field trip to the National Constitution Center. We went specifically to see a theater production called *Living News,* which was a short, smart play that showcased constitutional issues, such as freedom of speech, gun control, and student rights. The field trip and *Living News* were designed to pique learners' interest in the topics and motivate them to seek more information on their own (develop their personal learning-to-learn skills) and voice their own opinions (oriented toward action).

Following our field trip, I asked learners to consider what issues seemed important in America today. The goal was to identify current events or controversial topics that could connect back to the Constitution. I wanted to familiarize learners with the text of the Constitution and get them to deeply understand the immediacy of this foundational document. Through "Do Now" (or short introductory) activities and class discussions, we generated individual and class lists of issues. Learners then had to take topics from our list and find exactly which article or amendment either mentioned or related to the issue. Learners used the "Interactive Constitution" on the National Constitution Center's Web site to locate issues, using keyword and other search mechanisms.

We moved from this more cursory study of the document into the learners' culminating POU, which effectively required learners to develop and demonstrate learning in civics and literacy. Learners had to choose a current constitutional issue and write either a letter to the editor or produce a public service announcement on their topic. My intention was for the final product to communicate understanding of the issue and the constitutional supports for either or both sides of the issue, and to require learners to write for an authentic audience.

The project certainly was not without challenges, and the learners produced a wide array of final products. In many of the less successful POUs, learners did not connect their issue to a close study of the Constitution and instead just used the POU as a chance to spout their opinions. Clearly, some connections were easier to make—like Philadelphia's "stop-and-frisk" policy and the Fourth Amendment. For others, the connections were harder to find. Some wanted to know exactly where hot-button topics like gay marriage or the recession were located in the Constitution. They weren't satisfied by seemingly weak connections between equal protection and due process under the Fourteenth Amendment and marriage rights, and were similarly baffled by how to find constitutional support for the stimulus plan or employment issues. In their frustration, I could see that learners were beginning to understand the Constitution and how it is and is not relevant to current issues. I would argue that even if the final product lacked the intended level of rigor, the process in these cases involved in-depth, learner-driven study of the Constitution as a document.

Learners also produced some excellent POUs. They were eager to submit letters to the editor and present public service announcements that were passionately written and well-produced. In these POUs, I saw learners successfully exploring and explaining their issues and demonstrating clear understanding of the Constitution. Most notable was the way the most meaningful work produced was supported by, and in support of, developing competencies. In presenting a POU that showed a mastery of autonomous research and production, a learner proved she was proficient in personal learning and development. The most persuasive pieces (those written and filmed) gave learners a way to take courageous action, at times advancing unpopular or controversial points of view. These competencies, while not an intentional part of the unit plan or even an explicit part of my assessment rubric, were deeply integrated into classroom activities and the learning produced therein.

CREATIVITY AND DECISION QUALITY
AND PROBLEM SOLVING

When I announced that *Dreamgirls* would be SOF's first musical, I heard the same phrase mumbled over and over: "This is *not* going to happen." I heard it so often I began to mumble it too.

This refrain spoke to a larger problem at the school: constantly changing leadership had resulted in a lack of stability. Programs that began one year vanished the second; systems implemented one minute were overhauled the next. And, thus, like the foolish man in the Bible who built his home on a foundation of sand only to see it fall, any sense of agency our learners felt disappeared as their expectations for the future collapsed.

This lack of empowerment characterizes urban students across the country. Excluded from decision making and denied a voice, they feel no compelling reason to attend school. Attendance rates fall. Graduation rates plummet. These urban realities made my decision to do *Dreamgirls* a challenge. After all, how can one rehearse with a cast that is either absent or unable to stay after school because they work? Most comprehensive high schools in Philadelphia answer that question one way: you can't. But nobody was telling me that.

I knew we had one thing that most Philadelphia high schools did not: a period during the day called project time. Because we had been forced to move away from our project-based curriculum, time for projects had been reduced to this ninety-minute block. Projects were meant to be hands-on, specific, and relevant. And so, with attendance problems in mind, we decided to make *Dreamgirls* a credit-bearing, scheduled project. In other words, *Dreamgirls* would be a class.

From the start, the learners were excited by this *Dreamgirls* class. Some educators, on the other hand, were suspicious. "It's not really a class," one commented. Others offered advice: "You'd better have the kids write a paper or two, or you're going to get into trouble for not really running a class!" In any other school, they would have been correct; theater traditionally inhabits the realm of extracurricular activities, which give learners a fun experience but not much else. But since coming to SOF, I had been taught to question the traditions of education. So I asked, Why can't it be a class?

Before the advent of the modern school, with its lines of desks and talking-head teachers, students learned by doing. There were no textbooks, no lectures, and no classes. Rather, young people were apprenticed to a master, who showed them how to do a task and then gradually offered less and less help until the task was mastered. For the student, there was no wondering about how his learning would relate to his future: what he was learning *was* his future.

The process of creating a play is much like an apprenticeship. By opening night, the play's success lies in the hands of the actors who must now do what they have learned. An actor, in the end, must become the creator. She must own her work because she is the only one standing on the stage.

Nothing was easy about the *Dreamgirls* class: learners were suspended, fights were fought, lines were forgotten. But just before opening night, a new sense of ownership emerged both onstage and off. One learner who had fought about the need for rehearsals came to me and said, "I have to go memorize my lines! Are you sure we can't rehearse all day tomorrow?" In the technical theater section of the class, which was run by another educator, three girls who never had sewn before in their lives were making last-minute costume alterations. A first-year learner blossomed into the best stage manager I have ever had. And, as I was driving one crew member home, I asked him what he wanted to do with his future. "Be a theater major," he replied. He had never done a play before *Dreamgirls*.

Unlike traditional classes, where the connection between learning and life is often hidden, the *Dreamgirls* project, like others at SOF, sponsored the oldest and best kind of learning: it involved learners in a real-world process, ultimately shifting responsibility for its outcome to them. And while the class was no panacea for attendance woes, I did notice a pattern: chronically absent learners were making it to school on *Dreamgirls* class days. And the week of the show our attendance was 100 percent—save for one learner who took a half-day off because he wanted to shop for a better costume.

This story is not one of radical innovation. Many schools do musicals. Many learners in those musicals learn lessons about responsibility. This story is, rather, one of innovative thinking. We viewed the traditional idea of a class as limiting, divorced from the real world and from real learning. So instead of seeing theater as an extracurricular activity, as something distinct from classroom learning, we framed it as a class—in the oldest sense of the word. And because our learners knew that what they were learning could be used in their own lives, they invested in the class and came to see it as part of a future they had the agency to shape. Unlike other learners who say they want to be an engineer but cannot explain what an engineer does, learners in the *Dreamgirls* class said they wanted to be costume designers, stage managers, and actors—and they knew exactly what they meant.

One day in the last few weeks of school, after I had announced that the next year's production would be *The Wiz,* one learner called to me in the hall: "I *gotta* be in the show next year!" I asked him why. "I'm going to be an actor! And, Mr. Emerson, everyone knows the school play is where you learn how to be one."

FUNCTIONAL AND TECHNICAL SKILLS

Microsoft defines one who is proficient in the competency of functional and technical skills as "possessing required functional and technical knowledge and skills to do his or her job at a high level of accomplishment."[6] Technology is an extension of our hands and minds that is intended to make our lives easier and more efficient. Why should this idea be any different in a school? Shouldn't we make new technologies accessible to educators and learners? Many people assume that, because we have Microsoft as a partner and that we have access to cutting-edge technology throughout our school, we are a technology school that prepares our learners to be programmers and technicians. However, the technology that we and our learners have access to is there to enhance and enable our learning—not to drive it. SOF is a comprehensive neighborhood high school that tries to prepare our learners to achieve their dreams, and for what those dreams might look like in a society infused with technology.

To guide a learner to achieve proficiency of this competency, one must have a plan, just like in teaching any other skill. At SOF, we like asking fundamental questions that drive decision making. What does teaching and learning of functional and technical skills look like? Traditional education, true to form, has tried to answer this question with a one-size-fits-all approach. Typically, all learners take the same class with the same curriculum, which is derived from the same standards and uses the same content to do the same activities. We are asked often why we don't have a technology class to prepare learners for the plethora of technologies they will encounter throughout their learning experience at SOF. However, the question challenges the fundamental assumptions we make about the best way to educate people—do we believe education is a matter of just-in-case learning or just-in-time learning?

How often are adults put in a situation where they need to adapt to a new job or career, or even learn new skills in their current career? When this happens, they are not sent to a class where they have to master a given list of skills before they can start doing their job. People are essentially immersed in their new responsibilities immediately after accepting them; if there is any training, it may only last a short time. Employees' success does not generally depend on training but on support and guidance. Education in our schools should simulate this to some degree.

To us at SOF, technology is best learned within the context of application. Teaching learners how to use a piece of hardware or a software application without the context of a problem or project is rarely beneficial. When we teach a series of skills that is for later rather than now—that is, just-in-case learning—little is typically retained. Therefore, when you get to the application, the skills must be retaught. At SOF, we believe that rather than teaching technology skills as a separate entity, we must teach them within a project-based environment. This provides learners with a context in which they can apply the skills to solve a problem. We believe this is how you become proficient at technology and, more broadly, at all required skills.

To provide an example of this philosophy in action, I will describe an ongoing project called Help Desk. This class was designed specifically to create a learner-managed technology support staff at SOF. My experience with the process of creating this class uncovered weaknesses in my planning and preparation, leadership, guidance, and structure. But it also illuminated something I believe about education for which I had no empirical basis: people will step up and learn whatever skills they need if they feel they are valued and empowered.

From the beginning, I stressed the importance of this entire process being managed by the learners and not by me. Together we developed a list of problems that needed to be addressed, tools that needed to be purchased, and procedures that needed to be created. All they needed was a little help defining the role of a help desk and they were able to generate most of the ideas. From this brainstorming, they created a standard operating procedure using a shared OneNote notebook. They collaboratively edited this notebook to create a description of the first-ever School of the Future Help Desk.

After defining the process, the learners needed to master the specific skills of hardware and software troubleshooting. At first I would show them short film clips that were structured around preparing for an industry standard certification, but they retained very little content. Working with the SOF technology staff, we devised a plan to use laptops that had been damaged beyond repair to immerse the learners in the troubleshooting process. The learners were immediately engaged in seeing what made the laptops tick. They loved to disassemble the computers, but had no plan for reassembly. This failure was the most genuine learning experience I have ever seen in the classroom. They immediately saw the repercussions of not being able to reassemble an expensive piece of equipment. This challenge created a high level of engagement and resulted in a high level of proficiency in functional and technical skills. Almost the whole class was able to completely disassemble a laptop and then reassemble it without having extra pieces or screws—not an easy task. By the end of the class, the group worked collaboratively to piece together working components of the destroyed laptops to create a number of functional machines.

Teaching technology skills isn't as simple as standing in front of a group of people and telling them how to do things. Any individual who is highly proficient in a field of technology will tell you that their proficiency was attained through curiosity, engagement, and, for the most part, tinkering. People learn by using and doing, and to do that they must have strong internal motivation. To instill such motivation in our learners, we must first concentrate on creating an engaging environment in which they are able to use their hands, ask questions, and solve problems. Engagement is paramount in education—and at SOF.

CONTINUOUS, RELEVANT, AND ADAPTIVE

Every educator wants nothing more than to influence a learner. They want to watch that metaphorical lightbulb go on, and for their learners to make connections. They want to create lifelong learners. They want to inspire thoughts and ideas. They want, in short, to educate. While lightbulb moments are still possible, in our test-driven academic culture in America, the learning that happens in high school is unfortunately not often all that meaningful to our adolescents. When I entered graduate school for education, I had hopes of changing education in our nation and making it more meaningful—at least to my classroom of learners. However, when I encountered SOF and realized that its ultimate goal was schoolwide reform, I realized I would have the chance not just to make education meaningful in one classroom, but to have the opportunity to rethink education in public schools across Philadelphia. In other words, to make education meaningful to a city's population of adolescents. As such, I applied to work at SOF. Throughout the application process, I was intrigued by the three words I kept reading over and over again—that the education received and delivered at the school would be "continuous, relevant, and adaptive." At the time I thought they were just neat words; I had no clue that they would become the center of my professional career.

What do those three words mean to education at SOF? How do they define SOF? How can learning be continuous, relevant, and adaptive? What does that look like in a classroom? How does it translate to a whole school? Our visionary leader, the first chief learner, made it possible partially by embodying these very words. Every time we created a process, whether for report cards, scheduling, or assessing, she would ask us if it was continuous, relevant, and adaptive. As we were designing our learning engagements— our projects and POUs—she would be there to make sure we were keeping the notions of continuous, relevant, and adaptive in our minds. She was always ready to sit down with us to discuss our plans. However, despite our many discussions, I still struggled with the notion of how to educate in a manner that was continuous, relevant, and adaptive. I don't think I truly understood what it meant until my final learning engagement of the year, a project called Money and Rights (M&R).

Money and Rights was designed to examine the relationship between income, money, and power in the world, specifically, the rights money allows one to access. We were particularly concerned with the economic situation of Philadelphia, which was experiencing an economic boom. New buildings were going up left and right, and the city was undergoing a massive transformation. The neighborhoods of over 75 percent of our learners, West Philadelphia (where SOF was located) and Parkside, were changing rapidly, with a number of new shopping centers and a new museum being built in our backyard. How would that change the neighborhood? How would that affect our community? What was the relationship between economic activity and the quality of life in a neighborhood? These were the guiding questions the learners and I set out to study and answer. As their educator, my hope was to combine understanding from the core subjects of mathematics, social studies, and English to help learners discover the answers to these timely questions. The concepts and connections to the Pennsylvania State Standards that were examined in this project included taxes, local government structures, supply and demand, elasticity of demand, graphing, slope, percentages, entrepreneurship, monopolies, small business versus large businesses, statistics, and West Philadelphia history.

At the end of this learning engagement, as a culminating POU, learners were asked to design a business plan that would create a service or business that addressed a need in the community. Community needs were assessed through a learner-created survey, which was randomly disseminated earlier in the project to thirty-five community members. Learners were allowed to work in groups of four or five. Their business plans were required to include the following: a graph of what they anticipated their demand and supply to be, a description of their product or service, and how their plan would address a need in their community. This written plan was then turned into a PowerPoint presentation. Once the presentations and written plans were completed by every group in the class, we invited a panel of twenty community members to a "business expo," where each learner team presented its ideas. Our visitors were asked to vote on which plan they thought would best serve the needs of their community and would ultimately be successful in the neighborhood. The winning group was to receive an assessment of either proficient or advanced—the equivalent of a B or an A on a traditional assessment scale.

How was M&R an example of continuous, relevant, and adaptive learning in the classroom? It was continuous because it allowed learners to build on previous learning at every step. At the end, they had to pull their thoughts together into a comprehensive product that displayed their ability to apply what they had learned to a question or problem in a new situation. It was relevant because it addressed the needs of their community at the present time. Learners had the opportunity to think critically about their neighborhoods and community economics, political and social structures, and the rights they were afforded. M&R proved to be adaptive because it allowed learners to choose a need of the community that they found particularly compelling and then address it in a way that they saw fit. No two learners had to create the same final project or research the same need. Learners had a voice, and individual learning differences could be addressed throughout.

While I still had much to learn as an educator in that first year, by the end of this project I felt like I had truly executed what SOF promised to offer—continuous, relevant, and adaptive learning. Learners were engaged. Lightbulbs went on. Content and competencies were mastered.

CREATING UNDERSTANDING

Why is it important to share our reflections on teaching and learning at SOF in conjunction with reflections on SOF's progress and success? While we can't yet demonstrate a link between these projects and our much anticipated PSSA scores, as they have not been published, we do want to demonstrate the strong correlation we witness each day between project-based learning and our kids' heightened level of engagement and enthusiasm for learning. When we provide our learners with opportunities like those described in these anecdotes, we see them rise to the occasion and walk away with a unique set of competencies, a sense of ownership, and an understanding that transcends traditional content-driven instruction. While we struggle to measure this intangible energy, we feel it each day when learners rise to meet our high expectations—carrying out complex projects, addressing community needs, and demonstrating some of the same competencies required of us as adult professionals.

It is our sincere hope that what readers take away from this collection of stories is that learning and success can and must be measured in a continuous, relevant, and adaptive way, and that it is important to change the way we, as a society, think about learning. We must move from a one-size-fits-all content and teacher-driven concept to a dynamic and adaptive understanding of the process of learning. And we must adapt the ways we measure learning to match our relevant definition. At SOF, a learner proves that he or she understands a concept through a POU—which demands both mastery of content and the demonstration of proficiency in twenty-first-century competencies.

The importance of test scores cannot be denied; we at SOF certainly do not argue with that. However, it's critical to look beyond the numbers for something more. We believe we have only started the journey of creating an environment and community where learning is continuous, relevant, and adaptive. We know that we are in uncharted territory and will continue to strengthen and structure our approaches to teaching and learning over time. Credit must be given to our SOF families and partners, who stand beside us each step of the way. To our community, the story of SOF is one of hope, and one that shows us what is possible for the next generation of learners.

8

No Regrets

Reflections from the Inside

Mary Cullinane

WHAT IF?

In 2003, Microsoft and the School District of Philadelphia agreed to form
a partnership that would investigate, determine, and deliver a high school
equipped to prepare learners for the twenty-first century. The goal was to
build and redefine the norm for urban high school education. At the time,
Microsoft was considering investing in and creating a School of the Future
resource similar to the Home of the Future, a facility on Microsoft's campus where visitors can experience how technology might influence home
design. Philadelphia had not built a new school in more than twenty years,
and district CEO Paul Vallas was hired partly on a platform of capital expansion. During a meeting between Vallas and Microsoft's education general
manager, Anthony Salcito, the decision was made to build, in partnership, a
high school in Philadelphia.

February 13, 2008
Congressional Testimony by Mary Cullinane

Chairman Miller, Ranking Member McKeon, Members of the Committee:
my name is Mary Cullinane, and I am the Director of Education Innovation

and Business Development for Microsoft. I also bring the perspective of a former teacher, Director of Technology and administrator of a high school in New Jersey . . .

The School of the Future is a unique public/private partnership initiated in September of 2003 and based on the question "what if"—what if a committed school district, its surrounding community, and a leading technology company came together to design a high school—one that was scalable, could be replicated nationwide, built and operated on a standard budget meeting all state and district requirements . . . Today's children deserve learning communities that are inspirational, not just functional . . . We need to communicate a message that we understand the challenges, but that we are ready to take them on.[1]

Over a year ago, we had the opportunity to present our experiences of building SOF before the House Committee on Education and Labor. This testimony represented our first significant public reflection. Our reflection has continued, as have the lessons we have learned. Throughout the past six years, Microsoft has stood strong in its commitment to this goal. We have celebrated each important milestone—from the groundbreaking, to the curriculum summit, to opening day, and in the not too distant future we will celebrate graduation ceremonies for the first SOF class.[2] We continue to believe in the promise of our vision, and we have worked tirelessly to address its challenges. At times, however, I have wondered if we were really ready to take every challenge on.

With any great undertaking comes great opportunity for learning. During my congressional testimony, I stated, "We must permit learning communities to innovate. True innovators will experience success and failure. We must inspire others to do more than they think they can do, and we must call on a variety of stakeholders to make this happen."[3] Failure is part of this journey. But it is not the definition of this work.

The lessons that follow are artifacts from our exploration. Each one has provided great return on our investment, as they will allow others to gain from our experience. Lessons learned, many; regrets, none.

"All great things are simple, and many can be expressed in single words: freedom, justice, honor, duty, mercy, hope."
—WINSTON CHURCHILL

One year prior to the opening of SOF, I chose Winston Churchill's words to capture the enormity and the emotions of this project. Our effort, born from a desire to answer the question, "What if?" had weathered the many obstacles of inertia, policy, and status quo. While only one of many actors, I had the rare opportunity to experience this work from the inside, representing a company doing something it had never done, in a city searching for ways to fix what seemed like insurmountable realities. Yet SOF still held promise. More important, it was generating rich debate and an overall awareness of education reform. On November 28, 2005, I posted the following to the Microsoft SOF blog:

> For the past two years we have been working very hard to dissect the intricacies of urban education. We've done the due diligence. We've read the "must reads." We've participated in the education echo-chamber and we've "drilled down." "data-drove." "researched-based" ourselves until there was no other jargon left to use . . .
>
> The facts are often quoted. As our kids get older, their performance when compared to their international counterparts declines. In 5 years, 50% of teachers leave the profession. The District of Columbia spends more per student than any other district in the country yet finds itself at the bottom of the achievement lists. 28% of college freshmen must take remedial courses. It goes on and on and on . . .
>
> Yet all across America there are examples of it working. In every state a story of excellence can be identified and celebrated . . . producing our poets, our Nobel prize winners, our doctors, and our leaders. The problem exists when we turn our focus to produce consistency.
>
> I know people are going to read this and roll their eyes. I know when we go back to our offices the bureaucracies waiting for us will immediately slow our progress. I know money matters and politics rule. However I also know these are things we created and therefore they are things that we control . . .

> I don't know how many people will read this, but for those that do, be
> the one . . . Be the one that knocks on the door and says we can do this.
> It may happen one classroom at a time, one school at a time . . . but don't
> despair.[4]

Now, six years after our first thoughts were put to paper, the sentiment
of hope is still present. Bruised. Questioned. Debated. But still present.
The lessons gleaned from this work have had a positive impact on many.
Over two thousand people have visited SOF. Politicians, researchers, educators, and corporations have celebrated and questioned our efforts. As a
result, Microsoft launched the global Innovative Schools Program, which
supports the development of whole-school reform in more than fifteen
countries, soon to expand to over thirty-five thousand schools worldwide.
Many questions remain, however, as the realities of urban high school reform continue to threaten the promise of this work and weather our spirit
of hope. But it is these challenges that have yielded our greatest assets: the
lessons learned from our mistakes and victories.

LESSON ONE: MONEY AND TECHNOLOGY ARE GREAT, BUT PEOPLE ARE BETTER

Saturday, March 27, 2004—SOF Blog

We picked our architect. They are going to design the "School of the Future." I hope within the bricks and glass, found in the chairs and hallways,
will be the same spirit they brought to that interview room. I hope every
stone is laid with that passion in mind. I hope that when anyone opens the
doors, and steps inside, they feel it.

That will be this school's legacy. Not the computers, not the software,
not the technology. It will be a passion for learning found in the hearts and
minds of every teacher and student who walks the hallways. That's what I
hope for this school.

The announcement of SOF brought widespread attention in 2003. Many
articles predicted that it would yield educational offerings with unparal-
leled technical resources and gadgets, showcasing the power of technology

in the teaching and learning process. Assumed to be similar to High Tech High in San Diego and other efforts to highlight the infusion of technology, SOF was expected to be a demonstration site with limitless funding. With such a level of resources, success was guaranteed. Yet three years have passed, and we have proven most of these assumptions to be either wrong or misconstrued.

What we have learned from SOF is that technology has a role. It is an important piece of the reform pie. It can provide access to relevant materials and expertise. It can assist in performance analysis and allow data to influence instructional improvements. It can motivate and create efficiencies. It can act as an accelerant and increase the opportunities for communication and collaboration between home and school. To truly address the challenges facing our urban centers, however, we must look beyond technology and money. We must take a more holistic approach by focusing on people.

Over the past decade, we have seen many initiatives that lacked the necessary support and infrastructure required for the successful integration of technology in classrooms. Underfunded laptop initiatives, where states and districts provide laptop computers to students and teachers without technical support, collaborative infrastructures, or professional development are all too common. Clearly, a lesson from SOF is that technology cannot be applied in isolation. It should neither be seen as a single strategy for improving student achievement nor be measured that way.

By addressing multiple areas of innovation—technical architecture, instruction, community engagement, building design, and business management—SOF attempted to create a learning environment that offered the greatest chance for success rather than a technical solution for a nontechnical problem. Have we succeeded? I will leave the answer to researchers who will follow years from now, as I believe more time is needed to draw meaningful conclusions. What we have learned from this effort so far is clear: we can no longer be myopic innovators.

I can remember the opening day of SOF as if it were yesterday. After a brief ceremony outside the entrance to the school, learners were led into the gymnasium. Unbeknownst to them, the gymnasium was filled with over one thousand people, with music heralding their entrance and families standing in ovation. I stood in the back of the hallway, watching as the young men and women entered. I will never forget their faces. And I will never forget those who turned to their friends and said, "I can't believe someone did this for us." It was that sentiment—combined with a visionary chief learner—that fueled much of the success our first year. Unfortunately, our struggle to maintain such inspiration over the past three years has been one of our greatest challenges—and one that cannot be solved by technology.

Our lessons here are many, and although somewhat obvious, they are often overlooked. First, be bold. Take on more than just a technology initiative. Look to innovate in core organizational areas such as business management, community enrichment, building design, technical architecture, and instruction. For instance, think about how much training we require for those conducting interviews with potential staff. I constantly ask that question of education audiences, and other than being told what they may not ask, little or no training is offered. If we want to purchase a textbook or buy a project, we form committees, and in some instances we hire consultants and put out a hundred-page "request for proposals." Yet to procure our most important investment, educators, we hand applicants a few questions an hour before the interview and ask them to come back with their best lesson.

Second, seek out more than just products from corporate partners. Microsoft's greatest contribution to SOF has not been its technology; it has been our people. Last year, Microsoft COO Kevin Turner came to visit the school. After receiving an overview of the organization, he was given a tour by four learners. They asked him if he had ever met Bill Gates. They asked him how many people worked for him. They asked him if he would give them each an Xbox. Toward the end of the conversation, Kevin turned to them and said, "Don't ever forget, you can do anything you put your mind to, and your only limitations are the ones you give yourself." He then shared that he had started his career as a cashier and now has a boss by the name of Bill Gates.

LESSON TWO: KNOW THE M.O.T.I.V.E.

M = Motivation

O = Obstacles

T = Trends

I = Interest

V = Values

E = Environment

Saturday, March 24, 2007—SOF Blog

Most importantly I believe what I have said all along . . . there is no silver bullet. There isn't a single strategy that can be deployed that will solve our problems. However if we take a step back . . . continue to demonstrate the courage and patience necessary to see this work through . . . support the belief that change takes time . . . years in fact, then I think we have a chance.

In early 2004, we arranged a focus group of fourteen seventh-grade students from a local elementary school in West Philadelphia. We provided them with pizza and drinks and encouraged them to dream big. During the conversation, I picked up my cell phone and informed the students that Bill Gates was expecting my call. He wanted to know, if they could be assured of one thing at SOF, what it would be. I mentioned that Mr. Gates was fairly well off and would be able to support their request. The only requirement was that they all had to agree.

So for the next ten minutes, they chatted. Finally I asked for their decision. Confident I was going to be installing large LCD televisions in the bathrooms as a result, I began to go around the room. From the wealthiest man they had probably ever heard of, they wanted only one thing: to be safe. SOF has taught us many things. One of its greatest lessons, however, has been to understand the true impact of ignoring the needs of our customers.

Given the tremendous data available—on graduation rates, student achievement, and college graduation—one would imagine that our inclination would be to reflect on our customers and their needs. I do not believe this is always the case. Over the last three years, we have had many discussions regarding curriculum, standards, discipline, schedules, and dress codes. I believe that we have at times forgotten to focus on M.O.T.I.V.E.

SOF has demonstrated a need to better understand what motivates our kids, what their obstacles are, what their interests are, what their values are, and what the environment they must deal with is. Just as those seventh-grade students taught us a lesson, so can the ongoing investigation of these fundamental ideas. While we paid great attention to this in the planning stage, we need to do a better job of integrating reflection systemically into the organization.

While there are many examples of special-admit schools leveraging the power of technology and myriad cases of charter organizations yielding solid outcomes with minority and underserved populations, few take everyone. Most screen students and determine who will be fortunate enough to attend. SOF chose not to follow this model. Our goal was to demonstrate that by creating a learning environment that understood the M.O.T.I.V.E. of those it served, all students could succeed and have access to excellence.

The lesson is that such a vision brings great challenges. The reality of what exists outside the walls of SOF is at times inconceivable. It calls into question decisions made and expectations generated. However, this reality is our nation's greatest challenge. Because of this, we must continue to place greater attention on understanding learners' M.O.T.I.V.E. and providing support services and resources to address such realities. The engineering of a culture cannot be taken for granted or left to chance. As educators, we must constantly review the M.O.T.I.V.E. of our learners and adapt our learning environments accordingly.

LESSON THREE: INNOVATION SWIMS UPSTREAM IN THE RIVER OF STATUS QUO

Saturday, March 24, 2007—SOF Blog

So what have been the biggest challenges?

Well . . . the system. And I'm sure this comes as no surprise. And I don't want to suggest that people have not been supportive. They have. However the system prevents them from going to the edge. The system prevents us from being creative. The system supports the status quo, not innovation. The system gets in our way. The system is frustrating.

I said to Chairman Nevels one day . . . imagine in our schools, if innovation was swimming downstream. Imagine how much further we could travel and how much faster we could get there. Unfortunately, in urban education, this is far from the case. In urban education, innovation is swimming upstream, encountering tides of policy and practice that slow its pace and prevent it from moving forward. And those taking the trip . . . swimming upstream is tiring. Let me tell you!

However, we will continue to move on. We will continue to attempt to remove the calcification that exists on the arteries of our systems and we will focus on the kids. That's the plan.

I do not believe that Microsoft fully appreciated the gravitational pull of the status quo and the tendency to regress toward the mean. I do not believe that we recognized the strength of institutional policy. Over the past six years, we have developed a greater understanding of the challenges of systemic urban reform. And while there have been numerous occasions when we have questioned our decision to attempt this project within the traditional governance model, this experience has taught us the most. We wanted to address the hard questions, not the easy ones. Simply proving that urban education is hard is not necessary. Finding a way to fix it is.

Still, at every turn there was a challenge. A grading system that focused on proficiency rather than a numeric yardstick was challenged due to a computer system that only accepted letter grades. A report card that provided multiple forms of assessment in a nontraditional format was challenged due to college admissions counselors who could not interpret them.

A community based on achieving proficiency through projects that could span across years was challenged by the need for students to be able to transfer to other schools. A later start time was challenged by the realities of late-afternoon safety concerns, work schedules, and athletic contests. Each of these concerns was valid because it represented a true roadblock caused by current policies. For innovation to occur, therefore, we must be willing to adjust policy.

At SOF, for instance, we tried to create a vision where learners would not fail. It would be understood instead that they had simply yet to demonstrate proficiency and therefore would receive a designation of "not on the radar." Other designations included novice and advanced. These designations were based on a review of project outputs; they were quite descriptive and went beyond a letter grade. The issue was that they were hard to translate into the district system. SOF's argument was, if you are simply going to translate "not on the radar" to an "F," then what is the difference? Given the need for consistency in reporting and adherence to state policy, that kind of translation eventually occurred. Some students felt it was easier that way, since they did not have to "explain it to their parents." Others, though, said that grades made them feel there was no hope of getting better. As one student explained, "Once you get an F . . . it's an F. You're done. However, when I got a 'not on the radar' I felt as if I could still make it better and didn't feel like a failure." While adjustments have been made, we will continue to press this issue and encourage others to do the same. As more school systems reinvent their yardsticks of success, the gravitational pull to the traditional will become less and less.

From the beginning, we were learning how hard it was to open SOF. Political considerations based on location, the definition of the "catchment" area that would determine who would have access to the lottery, the materials permitted in the school building, construction delays caused by a limited availability of workers and city bureaucracy, internal organizational issues, and frequent personnel changes—we experienced all of them. However, what can never be lost was the presence of tremendously dedicated individuals, whose passion and perseverance overcame every challenge.

A critical lesson we learned was to be more prescriptive. When entering this type of partnership, organizations should clearly articulate what standard operating procedures will be. This articulation should be documented, reviewed, and revised throughout the length of the partnership. Furthermore, clear statements of nonnegotiable considerations should be outlined. While recognizing the fluidity and necessary ambiguity that will be encountered, substantial attention should be paid to those design elements that must remain constant.

Another important lesson we gleaned was to cast a broad net of influence. Since we began this partnership, we have seen the following leadership changes: the chief executive officer (2), the chief academic officer (2), the chief information officer, the chief of staff (3), the chief financial officer, the chief operating officer, the regional superintendent (2), the chief development officer, the chairman of the School Reform Commission (2), and the chief learner (3). While the transitory nature of education leadership is well documented, this turnover has presented clear challenges. Our ability to continue the mission was first crafted by a leadership team that is no longer in place. A successful public-private partnership requires the ability to transcend organizational adjustments and create an opportunity for long-term success. The fact that Microsoft is still here, working toward the original goals of this partnership, is a great testament to the strength of our vision.

Yet, certain realities remain. The suggestion of having a list of nonnegotiables that must be followed by new administrations is somewhat naive. Imagine walking into President Obama's office and saying, "But George promised." It is here where one of our greatest challenges resides. Given the change in leadership at the school, creating stability within the neighborhood or with partners was difficult. Such partnerships, however, could help organizations withstand changes in executive leadership at the district level.

Finally, success requires a strong and committed leader. Efforts like SOF will not be successful without the support and commitment of district leadership. In May 2004, I wrote:

> The past month has proven that without great leadership, innovation drowns.

As with any large organization, found within are different agendas, perspectives, beliefs, and personalities. These "differences" help to make organizations unique and can provide an opportunity to differentiate. However, they can also stop change and innovation dead in their tracks. So the trick . . . create an environment where individuals can thrive, but where the collective whole moves towards one common vision. That . . . takes great leadership.

Know that in times of changes and challenge, those around you need you to be more visible. Those around you need you to know when to calm the waters and when to ruffle the feathers. Those around you need you to set the vision and reiterate it as many times as necessary. Send email. Hang posters. Make buttons for cry'n out loud . . . even make people wear them! Do whatever it takes. Those being led . . . offer debate, challenge the course. But when the decision is made . . . when the course is set, get on board. Anything less is simply not fair to others around you.

The roadblocks created, the bureaucracy experienced, and the patience necessary requires committed and courageous leadership. Absent it, failure is assured. I put great hope in the current leadership of the School District of Philadelphia. I strongly believe that we are about to turn another corner. By improving communication and creating a stronger partnership, we will continue to grow as an organization and get closer to achieving our goals.

LESSON FOUR: USE A SHORT-TERM YARDSTICK FOR A LONG-TERM JOURNEY

Saturday, March 24, 2007—SOF Blog

We've welcomed over 50 countries to the School of the Future World . . . where we discussed the opportunities and barriers facing education today and tomorrow. We've traveled within the US and beyond talking about the school and why it matters. Articles have been written and movies made. Despite all of this attention . . . I'm still wondering. Have we done enough? Will this make a difference?

I must say, September 7th is a day I think about often. It was a day full of promise and absent were the traditional tensions of urban school systems. It was a celebration where people were proud and children were happy.

Few frustrations had been experienced yet. No budget crisis was looming. People were all focused on the same goal.

So where are we? Well, no matter where we go I get asked the same question. I find it very indicative of where we are as a country in our analysis of education . . . "What are the test scores showing?"

Michael Fullan, John Bransford, Jim Collins, and others have spent their careers researching leadership in organizations, how people learn, and what characteristics reflect success. One common element to this work is time and the consideration it deserves.

The tension between development time and determination of success has been present since the beginning of this project. Recognizing that these are kids—with futures, needs, and expectations—yet still trying to allow for adjustments and discovery along the way has been one of our greatest challenges. Given the constructs of our attempt—urban district, traditional budget, abiding district governance, neighborhood high school with no admittance requirement, constructivist learning methodology—three years is too little time to determine this project's success. And yet, in our schools around the nation, we use short-term yardsticks to determine the success of a long-term journey.

In 1998, Thomas Reeves conducted the study, *The Impact of Media and Technology in Schools*, which sought to "summarize the evidence for the effectiveness and impact of media and technology in K–12 schools around the world." In it, he refers to a multitude of research that has reviewed the effectiveness of technology in classrooms. It is his description of the Lehrer study of 1993 that offers great insight:

> Lehrer describes the development, use, and results of a hypermedia/multimedia construction tool called *HyperAuthor* that was used by eighth graders to design their own lessons about the American Civil War. This study exemplifies the principle that: "Cognitive tools empower learners to design their own representations of knowledge rather than absorbing knowledge representations preconceived by others."[5]

One group used these resources and one group did not. Upon completion of the study, both groups were given identical teacher-constructed tests. And what could be considered a surprise by some and be expected by others was that the outcome produced no significant test differences. However, what followed should make us reflect often on the short-term yardsticks we use to measure our success in education:

> However, a year later, when students in the design and control groups were interviewed by an independent interviewer unconnected with the previous year's work, important differences were found. Students in the control group could recall almost nothing about the historical content, whereas students in the design group displayed elaborate concepts and ideas that they had extended to other areas of history. Most importantly, although students in the control group defined history as "the record of the facts of the past," students in the design class defined history as "a process of interpreting the past from different perspectives."[6]

Outcomes of significance take time to measure. I hope that we will be able to continue the work of SOF. I hope that the challenges experienced these first three years will not be the full body of work on which we will be judged. And I hope that we consider the tremendous impact of the constraints that we chose to work under.

Some observers may ask what makes this school so different. It is a fair question. But my answer may be somewhat surprising. Our goal was never to be "so different." Our goal was to figure out a way where success could be found in the norm, not the exception. Our goal was to demonstrate that public-private partnerships can improve both organizations and generate additional resources to support education. Many say this work is not reflective because the might of Microsoft cannot be replicated everywhere. I disagree. Every community has strong private-sector organizations with amazing people and great resources.

It does not take a Microsoft, or an Apple, or an IBM. It takes organizations that can provide committed people and resources in a thoughtful and systemic way. To encourage this, for example, required internships for learners could yield tax relief for corporations. Or, free use of internal training resources and leadership development tools at companies could be made available to local educators for free. What makes SOF unique is the process used to create innovation and the commitment to develop and sustain it. Together with a rigorous and relevant environment—available to all, without selection—such attributes are worthy of consideration.

There are several lessons on this count. First, partnerships of this type require a strong articulation of principles. Length of time, level of involvement, effect of organizational changes, and budgetary adjustments must all be discussed in detail and articulated publicly. These considerations require constant review and adjustment. They must reside in a living document that is shared broadly and freely. Not knowing how hard this was going to be gave us the sense that this was unnecessary. Now knowing how hard it is, such necessity could not be clearer.

Second, we should share small achievements loudly and often. As the organization and culture began to develop at SOF, there were many instances of success. While taking different forms, these illustrations represented outcomes beyond traditional achievement scores. Stories of increased student participation, improved communication styles, enhanced parental involvement, and new interests in learning were taking place every day. We should have shared them internally and externally. Success breeds success. By creating a momentum of inspiration, we could have solidified our culture sooner and brought about greater stability.

Third, we should train school leaders to develop political acumen. Leaders have to communicate and lead those within their building. They also need to communicate and interact with their external communities. We did a poor job of ensuring that we were as connected to the district as to our immediate constituents. Such navigation almost becomes a true art form and is one that we must do a better job of developing in school leaders.

LESSON 5: SO MANY LESSONS, SO LITTLE TIME

Sunday, September 3, 2006—SOF Blog

In 5 days, this school is going to open and I couldn't allow that to happen without some reflection. So . . . what have we learned?

People first . . . everything else later. As a result of this project, I've been interviewed by a fair share of reporters. I've given a few speeches, and have spoken with educators from around the world. And there is nothing that I am more certain about than this . . . The School of the Future will open on September 7th because we had the right PEOPLE on the project. They were passionate, focused on kids, willing to try new things and worked harder than ever. Finding the right people . . . getting them on board . . . and then helping them cross the finish line is how great things happen. And it is certainly what allowed this school to open.

This is hard. It shouldn't have been this hard. It shouldn't take a miracle to build a great school in an urban community. It shouldn't be an exhausting experience, leaving participants tired and frustrated. It needs to be easier. We need more agile learning organizations. We need to figure out a better balance between control and creativity. We need to create an environment that is inspirational, not just functional. We need governance structures and public policy that set high standards, but also provide resources to achieve them . . .

You have to ask the question. If you want to bring reform . . . ask. If you want to try something new . . . ask. If you want to change the status quo . . . ask. This project would never have come to fruition if Paul Vallas hadn't ask the question, "What if". 9 out of 10 times, the answer will probably be no. But if that one time the response returned is yes . . . all the years of being turned down just became worthwhile.

It's the journey . . . September 7th will be amazing. But it will pale in comparison to the moments experienced over the past three years. I'm pretty sure I will never have the opportunity to be part of something like this again. (I don't think I'll be up to it) However, the past three years have been the chance of a lifetime. I hope I have served it well.

It is interesting to reflect on these lessons. Learned before a student ever stepped foot in the building, they characterize frustration, hope, and determination. Now, three years after opening day, while these same emotions are present and the lessons are richer, it is worth asking, what would we do again?

1. *Try.* This was the right thing to do at the right time. The challenges facing education today cannot be solved by education alone. Public-private partnerships must contribute to our efforts if we are to succeed in the twenty-first century. Do not fall victim to those who will

criticize your effort. If the solution is so apparent, why are they not out there doing it?

2. *Focus on process.* Over the past three years, we have shared the process by which we built SOF with thousands of people. Using the lessons that we have learned, districts and organizations have benefited from investigating our approach and leveraging it where appropriate. Assets developed, such as the Education Competency Wheel and the 6I Development Process, have been consumed and valued by educators worldwide. Perfect? No. Worthy of consideration? Yes.

3. *Limit exceptions.* Each time a visitor would come to SOF and hear the decisions we made prior to the partnership, heads would nod. We followed a traditional budget, acceded to union contractual requirements, and abided by state assessments. Each of these considerations allowed others to believe that our journey could support their efforts. Too often, innovative learning environments are the exception. While it was difficult, building SOF under traditional constraints provides us with a tremendous body of knowledge.

4. *Do it where it is hard.* Creating SOF in Philadelphia, an urban school district with a history of hardship and struggle, has afforded this project extraordinary credibility. And despite those who point to this decision to work under a traditional governance model as a design flaw, we point to our nation's reality. In our country today, one kid drops out of school every twenty-nine seconds, and students in urban locations are twice as likely to do so than their nonurban counterparts. While frustrating at times, many have looked at our attempt in Philadelphia as a strong indicator that success is possible even in the toughest circumstances. Perseverance, however, is required.

5. *Involve the community.* While we can still improve our efforts greatly in this respect, our focus was accurate. Leaders come and go. Partnerships dissolve. Programs lose funding. West Philadelphia, however, is here to stay. For true reform to take hold and remain strong and consistent through inevitable periods of change, the community must be central.

What do we wish we had done differently?

1. *Not lose our leader one year after the school opened.* While unfortunately out of our control, this transition influenced our work greatly, especially since the school had yet to solidify its culture. This affected the learners, the staff, and the community. It is only now, with the current chief learner in place, that we have begun to reengineer the community to reflect our original vision for the school. We should have built a stronger support network for leadership. We also underestimated the stress and requirements of the job. Leadership support teams and professional communities should be a requirement of every reform effort that finds its way into public school districts.

2. *Not assume that project-based learning alone could address the needs of all students.* While still committed to the promise of project-based learning, our community needed greater opportunities for remediation. Stronger benchmark analysis, student mentors for every learner, and extended-day opportunities for remediation should have been mandatory.

3. *Improve orientation for those who entered the community after year one.* So much of our success was the result of individuals understanding and believing in our vision. As new educators and learners entered the community, we should have provided them with the history and values of the organization. We assumed that everyone understood what had occurred prior to the school's opening. We did not realize how important opening day was for our learners and therefore did not predict the its impact on those who did not experience it. The adjustments made in this area have been significant and we believe will yield great improvement.

4. *Ensure identification of a senior liaison between the district and Microsoft.* This partnership began with the School District of Philadelphia identifying a senior leader as its point of contact for SOF. This individual and I work together daily to support the development of the school. With direct access to the Microsoft CEO, this liaison was able

to steer the tides of policy and practice in the district and alleviated many challenges. Stacey Rainey, a member of our team and a full-time Microsoft employee, assumed responsibility for this project as part of her portfolio after the school opened. Her continued dedication has enabled Microsoft to navigate the tremendous change that has occurred over the past three years. However, we have lacked a counterpart for her at the district. Now, with new leadership in place, the chief academic officer Dr. Pitre has identified herself as our point of contact, and we have already seen great improvement.

5. *Do not underestimate the tendency to retreat toward the norm.* Status quo has amazing gravitational pull. Add periods of leadership transition, and what is sure to follow is a regression toward what has always been. While I still believe in our goal of working within the normal structure of an urban district, our attempt has been made more difficult as a result. If following in this footstep, plan for a difficult journey. Consider a transitional phase in which new schools provide a formal environment that supports deviation from the mean. Such structure should be public and rigorous. Once norms and success are established, the organization can be removed from the temporary "shelter" and placed into the "normal" governance model.

Saturday, March 24, 2007—SOF Blog

Hi everyone! As I sit here and reflect that it has been more than 6 months since the School of the Future has opened, I am constantly reminded that this is a work in progress, as are all great challenges. And while the journey has taken many different turns, I'm glad to report that the most important characteristic of this work still exists . . . hope.

I will never regret Microsoft's involvement in this work. I will look back over the past six years as some of the most rewarding of my life. I thank Anthony Salcito, my manager, for giving me the opportunity to participate in this effort. Without his vision, none of this would have been possible. I also applaud every educator, parent, and learner who has contributed his or her passion. We are still here. After six long years, we are still bringing energy to the city of Philadelphia and the children it serves. Microsoft employees like Stacey Rainey and Tony Franklin wake up every day thinking about and interacting with SOF. They remain committed to its success and demonstrate our greatest contribution.

Reviewing elements of SOF that are different from the norm might seem inconsequential and lacking in innovation. However, their collective nature is powerful. To this day, I believe we are building a school of the future. I believe that it is a journey that never ends, and I believe that we have developed a tremendous foundation that will lead to success. I do not think that we are merely experimenting. In fact, I believe one could argue that an effort that yields less than a 66 percent success rate for children of color should be considered experimental.[7]

While we are not made up of a selection of the "best and the brightest," we serve a contingent representative of where our country is failing—those who are being left behind because they were not "selected" or fortunate enough that their parents would commit to participation or "special enough" to be availed of great personal attention to their gifts and talents. We are trying to figure out how we can best prepare "everyone else" for the future.

Our hope is that others will try. Our hope is that every school in America becomes a School of the Future, characterized not by the technology within its hallways, but by the passion for learning within the hearts of its students.

9

Lessons Learned

Technology, Reform, and Replication

Chester E. Finn Jr.

SCHOOL OF THE FUTURE is an appealing educational institution that many teenagers would find a swell place to attend secondary school.

Not everyone, to be sure. It is in an iffy neighborhood and is too small to boast every imaginable course, sport, or extracurricular activity. Some people do not thrive under its "progressivist" regimen of teaching and learning.

But it has a lot going for it: an awesome facility; committed educators; ample resources; sustained help and involvement from one of the world's most successful companies; and tons of nifty technology, including a laptop for every student—one they can even take home.

Nobody can yet be certain about the school's results, however. The first class will graduate in 2010, so we have little idea what their subsequent education and life trajectories will look like. As I write, the first round of state accountability testing is at hand. SOF's emphasis on project-based learning is awkwardly aligned with Philadelphia's curriculum and Pennsylvania's assessments. And there has been plenty of turnover among students, as well as in the school and district leadership.

Like the adolescents enrolled in it, SOF abounds in both promise and uncertainty. Today, however, it cannot be termed a proven success, a school that reliably produces solid academic results and collateral social benefits in interesting ways and at a manageable cost.

But giving SOF the benefit of the doubt, let us assume that its results turn out to be good. So what? Gratifying as it always is to come across a commendable school that does well by disadvantaged youth, in and of itself that probably would not justify this chapter, much less the larger volume of which it is a part. America has dozens of impressive one-off schools. Our problem is that the country craves hundreds or even thousands of them, and what therefore makes an outstanding school truly interesting is the possibility that it—or at least its key ingredients—might be scalable.

The holy grail of U.S. education reform is replicating success, not emulating truffle hunters by spotting one more solid school. It is figuring out how to change the life prospects of large numbers of children by creating and successfully operating—year in and year out—large numbers of high-impact schools.

In recent years, that quest has often led to the launch of ventures by entrepreneurs dedicated to creating "break-the-mold" schools and systematically replicating them.

That is no oxymoron. America needs new education molds to replace the ones that have failed. It is fine to start with a single new school that works. But if all we can learn from it is that a bunch of remarkable people came together to do something good for one set of kids in one place at one time—well, we should definitely applaud them, but in reality we will not derive much wider benefit. What America needs most is the kind of education accomplishment that can be transformed into a new mold in which many strong schools can be formed and scattered across the land.

We ought not to expect this national mission to be embraced with passion or skill by any single school system or state. Their proper concern is with their own students, not those a thousand miles away. We would also be foolish to count on the elaborate infrastructure of establishment institutions that serve districts and states (e.g., colleges of education, publishing companies, professional associations, teachers unions) to play lead roles in developing and replicating new schools. Entrenched quasimonopolies are almost never capable of such innovation. (Consider recent events in the Detroit automobile industry.) And myriad restrictions on the use of public funds—not just in education—make it exceptionally difficult to deploy tax dollars in the flexible yet precise fashion that we associate with venture capital. No, if we hope to find this sort of creativity, investment capacity, openness to innovation, and zeal to propagate success, we must look to entrepreneurial initiatives and individuals.

The purpose of this chapter is not to appraise SOF's educational offerings, laud its technology, judge its performance, diagnose its shortcomings, or predict its future. My mission is to place SOF in the context of that entrepreneurial strand within U.S. school reform that has sought to create and reproduce innovative schools that reliably succeed with underprivileged youth on a significant scale. We do not have many such examples, but they include the well-known Knowledge Is Power Program, the Core Knowledge Foundation, Aspire Public Schools, Achievement First, and at least a few more.

I have been involved in various ways with three earlier ventures that shared this aspiration. I took part in the brainstorming team that helped Lamar Alexander and David Kearns to develop the New American Schools Development Corporation (later New American Schools). I was a founding partner of Chris Whittle's Edison Project (now EdisonLearning). And I was a founding board member and chair of the education advisory committee for K12 Inc., the Bill Bennett-Lowell Milken virtual-school company.

Each of these initiatives was very different. New American Schools raised philanthropic dollars to underwrite a competition among nonprofit school-development teams to devise rival models that public school systems were then expected (with the help of federal money) to embrace. Edison deployed private venture capital to finance a profit-seeking effort to invent a single, modern, replicable school design that Whittle first planned to grow into a chain of private schools, then modified into a blend of public charter schools and privately managed district schools. K12 is also a profit-seeking firm that used private investments to develop an online curriculum and instructional program that parents homeschooling their children could purchase directly. It also launched a national network of "cyberschools," most of which operated as statewide charter schools, and has recently begun to offer its wares as supplemental programs for district-operated schools.

SOF differs sharply from all these because—so far as I can tell—it never overtly aspired to be more than a single, district-run public school. It did not set out to be a chain or network. But nor was it a random meteor. From the standpoint of one of its organizational parents, the School District of Philadelphia, it was a promising example of a new genre of high school—innovative, small, start-from-scratch, undertaken in partnership with respected outside organizations. For its other parent, the mighty Microsoft Corporation, it was to be a showcase where the world could glimpse not only technology's potential to transform teaching and learning but also what might be accomplished by using the products, insights, and strategies of Bill Gates's company. Both parents, in other words, saw SOF as a solitary heavenly body—but one endowed with rare powers to pilot, demonstrate, and ultimately help transform a larger cosmos.[1]

THE DNA OF SOF

National Developments

Besides its parents, SOF had numerous ancestors and relatives. Indeed, its gene pool incorporates five big trends in American education and six unique circumstances that converged in Philadelphia around 2002.

1. *Deepening interest in high school reform.* For two decades after the National Commission on Excellence in Education declared the United States "a nation at risk," much attention was paid to elementary and middle schools, which led to modest upticks in scores on national and international assessments. States channeled much of their education reform energy into grades K–8 and so did the federal government, particularly in the 1994 reauthorization of the Elementary and Secondary Education Act and the 2002 version known as No Child Left

Behind. High schools, however, proved stubbornly resistant to reform, and their results—whether measured in test scores, graduation rates, or college readiness—remained essentially flat. By the early twenty-first century, education-reform groups such as Achieve, policy leaders such as the National Governors Association, and major funders (notably Bill Gates's own foundation) were turning their focus to high school reform.

2. *The creation of start-from-scratch, innovative, smallish schools, usually with unaccustomed independence from traditional districts, many of them schools of choice.* American education was gradually weaning itself from the assumption that schools are immortal institutions. Rather, a school could be created de novo from a purposeful design, as illustrated by the emergence of thousands of charter schools in dozens of states; the work of New American Schools, which held its design competition in 1992; and the federal Comprehensive School Reform Program, often referred to as Porter-Obey, which underwrote the spread of many such school models.

3. *Widening use of technology in education.* Although technologies of many kinds—from chalkboards to overhead projectors to television—are familiar elements of U.S. schools, by the early twenty-first century the education system was also warily experimenting with more sophisticated applications of information technology, computers, telecommunications, and the brave new world of the Internet. (The federal subsidy for schools to access the Web—known as E-rate—began in 1996.)

4. *Outsourcing of school functions—even the operation of entire schools—to private organizations, as well as all manner of partnerships between public schools and a menagerie of outside entities.* Public education was no longer seen as the exclusive mandate of public-sector employees working for government bureaucracies. (Partnering has been going on forever, but the first full-fledged outsourcing of public school operations began in 1992, when Baltimore entered into a management contract with Education Alternatives, Inc. [E.A.I.], to run a dozen of its schools.)

5. *Leveraging private resources to augment public funding and expertise.* Here, too, the taxpayer had stopped being the sole source of public school resources. This development went far beyond magazine sales, carnivals, and other traditional raisers of small discretionary sums for schools and their PTAs. Now it included the half-billion-dollar 1993 gift of Walter Annenberg, the mounting munificence of Eli Broad, the Gates Foundation, and hundreds of other national and local funders, not to mention the outside brainpower and technical assistance by groups ranging from the Coalition of Essential Schools to Standard & Poors.

Philadelphia: Specific Circumstances

All of those national trends have endured—and, indeed, intensified—in American education, but in and of themselves they do not cause anything to happen in a particular place. Action only occurs where the local stars are also aligned, as happened in Philadelphia from 2002 to 2006, when SOF was conceived, planned, and built. Six elements were key:

1. In late 2001, the Commonwealth of Pennsylvania effectively seized control of the city's deficit-riddled, poorly performing public school system and assigned responsibility for it to a new School Reform Commission (SRC), with members appointed by the governor and mayor. This unusual governance arrangement conferred sweeping powers on the SRC, and at least partly insulated its members from the local political influences and interest groups that typically block change in urban school systems.
2. Chaired by the determined and foresighted James Nevels, a successful investor, banker, and attorney, the SRC quickly recruited the high-powered, hyperkinetic Paul Vallas from Chicago to Philadelphia to take charge of the school system. He arrived in summer 2002, bent on confirming his reputation as a successful urban-education reformer.[2]
3. Vallas's reform agenda included an immediate push to launch small, innovative high schools in partial replacement of the city's traditional

but faltering behemoths, and a portfolio approach to school management that featured both charter schools and the outsourcing of dozens of district schools to private managers.[3]
4. A gritty West Philadelphia neighborhood that needed a shot in the arm—what could be better than a new school to function as an anchor institution, housing various community services and helping to catalyze larger renewal efforts?
5. Microsoft's interest in building a model high-tech school to boost its visibility in the education market, much as it had done with a Home of the Future on its main Seattle campus. That the school turned out to be in Philadelphia was due in no small part to the charismatic Vallas, but SOF's access to essential outside resources—money, talent, and expertise—was due principally to Microsoft.
6. A teachers union contract made it easier in Philadelphia than in most cities to confer personnel independence on a new school—that is, one with the authority, under certain circumstances, to decide for itself who would teach in it.

RISKS AND RESILIENCE

Aligned stars are essential for innovations to occur. The risk for new and unconventional schools, however, and a hazard for education reform in general, is that stars move. No alignment lasts long, so a crucial question is whether an innovation can become sufficiently embedded in the "system" while it is aligned so that it has a decent shot at continuing once the alignment goes askew. (That is doubly important if the innovation is ever to be cloned or reproduced.) This turned out to be a challenge for SOF.

The peripatetic Vallas left Philadelphia for New Orleans in 2007, and Nevels left the SRC the same year. Neither of their successors was particularly bullish about SOF, and their reform strategies and leadership styles were quite different. This left SOF vulnerable to being recaptured and denatured by the school system, particularly when key Vallas lieutenants also exited.

That remains true today, and SOF devotees have additional jitters about academic performance. What will happen to the school's backing if assessments indicate that its pupils are not learning enough? There is also concern about student turnover (as is the case throughout Philadelphia high schools), which exacerbates the worry over academic results. And there is concern about the community's and the school system's patience while an innovation like SOF takes the time to work out its kinks, complete its design, and prove itself.

This volume is partly intended to foster such patience and sustain hope. (It was also an unusually gutsy invitation for candid midcourse feedback, even if that proved slightly uncomfortable for those striving to ensure SOF's success and reputation.) Yet SOF's very structure and birthing amplify its vulnerability. With the best of intentions, its founders sought to show that such an innovative school could succeed with the regular kids found in a challenging urban district—and that this could be done "within the system." They did not want a selective school. They did not want a charter or outsourced school or other special governance arrangement. And they opted to start with a high school, which everyone knows is a greater challenge than beginning with young children.

These are all worthy intentions. But every one of those decisions added to the innovation's precariousness and, in the end, left it urgently needing precisely the sorts of interventions and protections that the founders had opted not to build into its basic structure. Indeed, one might well say that the insistence on innovating via a "regular" school—a high school, open to all, in a tough neighborhood, governed in the usual way, with no constitutional protections or security guarantees—was naïve if not reckless.

In some ways, of course, SOF was not a regular school at all—and I am not just referring to its dazzling technology. Fundamental to its launch—its site selection, its physical design and construction, its emphasis on project-based learning, its budget and staffing, and its hardware and software—were high-level political support within the school system as well as the wider Philadelphia community, millions of dollars in private fundraising, the deep involvement and assistance of Microsoft, and a handful of dedicated individuals who nurtured it (and still do).

Continuity of something this unconventional and expensive is an immense challenge. That would be so even if the original rainmakers were still in place and is obviously more so in the wake of their departure. Yet the founders opted not to construct any of the obvious breakwaters that would help it withstand changing political tides and pressure to conform.

School systems generate many such pressures, and the larger the district, the more intense the pressure. Whether it is teacher credentials, annual calendars, daily schedules, transportation arrangements, homework policies, core curricula, standardized tests, identical textbooks, compatible software, or just a citywide cafeteria menu that can be published in the newspaper, the district pushes hard on all of its schools to be alike in crucial ways, even when it may simultaneously declare that they are different and that people can choose among them.

Such pressures have plagued SOF from the beginning, as they do any unconventional school or program. Resisting them—and winning the requisite exceptions, waivers, and special alternative arrangements—has presented daunting hurdles and still does today. The question is how to sustain nonconformity in an environment that engenders and rewards conformity.

Making this challenge even more difficult, however, is what we might term its very obverse: leadership instability, both at the system level (Vallas, Nevels, etc.) and in the school chief learner's office. At SOF, that office was occupied by three different people during the school's first three years. Such turnover is a major handicap for any school and worse for an innovative startup with no track record, no loyal alumni, and no compelling traditions.

The change of chief learners was partly bad luck. The first occupant—hand-picked by the school's planners a year in advance, intimately involved with SOF's design, development, and initial staffing, and reportedly well-suited to the post—experienced family issues that made it necessary for her to leave Philadelphia prematurely. It was the appointment of the second chief learner that demonstrated the school's vulnerability to changes and pressures beyond its walls.

The system first installed an interim school head, a retiree who "really didn't get" what SOF was about. Then (in the leadership vacuum arising from Vallas's departure) an "area superintendent" ignored the results of a careful search process and instead appointed someone whose experience was in elementary schools and who did not understand the singularities of SOF. "By the end of the year," I was told, "everyone realized she had to go," and the school's allies and strategists, likely including Microsoft, persuaded the system to offer her a position downtown. The third chief learner is reportedly doing fine, but as I write she has not yet completed even one full year on the job.

This kind of turnover in the front office could wreck the best of established schools, much less an unconventional start-up. In the case of SOF, what kept leadership instability—along with a hundred pressures from the district to conform to citywide norms—from doing major damage was the project's powerful informal support system: the involvement of Microsoft, influential private donors, a well-disposed mayor, and several remarkable individuals who have been relentlessly devoted to the school.

Yet the school had no constitutional authority to settle any of these things for itself. It had no charter or contractual right to self-governance. Its freedom to be different—even to continue, much less to grow, prosper, and spin off lessons or clones—depended on the will of the Philadelphia school system. Given the revolving-door leadership and "spinning wheels" strategies of large urban school districts, in retrospect it seems short-sighted that SOF's founders installed no institutional mechanisms to vouchsafe the school's long-term integrity. It does not even have a high-status advisory committee of influential community members who can pick up the phone to persuade officials and enforcers to make exceptions. That is no way to build a strong, secure, and durable institution that can continue to go against the grain of a large public-sector bureaucracy in a highly political environment.

TO REPLICATE OR NOT TO REPLICATE?

Although replication is the polestar of most serious education reformers, cloning SOF was never the explicit goal of its founders. From day one, Vallas and Nevels and their colleagues intended SOF as a unique one-off—a single flower within a mixed bouquet of new schools affiliated with various partners rather than a model to be copied. Its launch owed much to proving a reform theory that was specific to Vallas and Philadelphia at the time. Although that theory entailed cultivating many distinctive flowers, none was meant to evolve into a hillside of identical blossoms.

Microsoft also did not view SOF as the first of an oven full of cookie-cutter schools. It is a software firm and had no interest in running or being responsible for schools. It did, however, need a showcase. Primary-secondary education is potentially a giant consumer of its wares and services, but developing and exploiting any market means having persuasive marketing materials—and in this field nothing is more compelling than a living, breathing school. That meant ensuring that SOF was an awesome educational institution, not just at its birth but also as it matured. Hence, it was in Microsoft's interest not only to invest financial and human capital in SOF, but also to shield it from the vicissitudes of the Philadelphia school system's practices, policies, and people that might spoil the model. In return, the company's resources, experts, and political clout have proven enormously valuable to SOF. The mutual benefit is obvious. But no company would want to shoulder such obligations in lots of places—and SOF's tribulations likely reinforced that view within Microsoft.

That the project itself landed in Philadelphia was adventitious, even opportunistic. Pre-SOF, Microsoft had not been particularly active in the school market, which was generally seen as Apple territory. (Of course, Bill Gates and his foundation have been much engaged in the K–12 reform arena.) As a result, the firm had neither a deep presence in any one school system nor an obvious place to put its prototype. As its interest in this big and potentially lucrative market quickened, it plainly needed a demonstration site.

Instead of dummying up a "school of the future" with no students in Seattle, company executives were persuaded by Vallas to create a real-world model in Philadelphia, where he was experimenting with new small high schools run in conjunction with well-regarded outside entities. It turned out that Microsoft and Vallas's interests dovetailed.

Still, SOF is more a beta site for Microsoft than something to be reproduced directly. A company veteran insists that theirs "is not a McDonalds approach." Rather, they have distilled a few successful processes from the SOF experience—notably the 6I Development Process, by which the school was developed, and the Education Competency Wheel by which its staff was selected—and they now make these available for free to interested people and schools via three-day Microsoft Institute training modules.[4] They say that they have learned from the SOF experience that educational technology is not the hard part; what is truly difficult is planning, implementing, and staffing something as radical as a new school model—an insight to which we return below.

Microsoft has plenty of education software and services available for purchase and use by school systems, and it has many U.S. customers and clients. But no more full-fledged Microsoft-branded schools can be found on American shores. One wonders if company executives concluded from the SOF experience that it might encounter warmer climates abroad, because they have moved from SOF to catalyze more than fifteen "innovative schools" in other lands, which also—as far as I can tell—serve more as demonstration sites than as something to be cloned.[5]

ANTECEDENTS AND ANALOGUES

Microsoft is in this market for the long haul. It does not need to rush, does not depend on K–12 education as a primary revenue source, and does not want to make major mistakes. It can afford to give away some appetite-whetting products and services, even to train people for free, if such offerings build loyal customers. Though it is not replicating SOF per se, it is using the lessons learned there, and the school's demonstration value, as part of a broader strategy for the education market.

That is very different from the experiences of three earlier efforts—two of them ongoing—by entrepreneurial organizations hoping to bring large-scale change to U.S. primary-secondary education by developing innovative schools, then reproducing them in quantity. Interestingly, their missions more closely resemble the efforts of the Gates Foundation than of the company that produced the Gates fortune. Their stories are instructive, however, if one believes that the slippery grail of replication is worth trying to grasp.

New American Schools. NAS faced four difficulties—and gradually died. First, it rounded up the "usual suspects" to devise break-the-mold models, an obvious contradiction in terms. NAS did not set out to do this; it staged a design competition that others could have joined—and some did. But the winners, likely because of a screening and selection process that tended to favor conventional thinking about education, yielded that result.[6]

Second, once the school-design process was complete, NAS and its winning design teams relied almost exclusively on established public school systems and states as customers. This was limiting, frustrating, and a source of compromise and incomplete implementation.

Third, because it started with the goal of innovation for its own sake, which led to multiple models, and because it became entangled with federal comprehensive school reform funding for its propagation, NAS had no unique educational franchise, no single conceptual flag to wave, and no good answer to the question, "Why not this other model, too?" In time, states were using their federal Porter-Obey dollars to pay for more than 250 different designs, most of them with no NAS affiliation, obviously leading to dilution—mockery, even—of the strategy, and eventually to its demise.

Fourth, NAS got going just as states were also installing standards, assessments, and accountability arrangements and as America was coming to judge its educational innovations more on the basis of academic performance. Yet RAND's careful evaluations of NAS basically found that its schools were producing no better results than the older models they more or less replaced.[7]

NAS began outside the system, as a privately funded venture. Yet the schools that its design teams devised could only be implemented within the system, and faithful implementation of unusual school models proved daunting. More and more compromises were made, even as Washington failed to put limits on which designs qualified for federal subsidy. The organization known as New American Schools no longer exists. And if one checks on the remaining "design teams" that it spawned, one finds, for example, that the Modern Red Schoolhouse now terms itself a provider of "technical assistance to districts and schools." Atlas Communities "partners closely with schools to develop and implement a comprehensive, multi-year plan for school transformation." America's Choice "helps districts and schools focus on five critical elements of school improvement." In other words, they all now function as consultants, advisors, and service providers to public schools and school systems. The system is their client and their revenue source. They are probably doing some good. What they are not doing is replicating large numbers of highly effective break-the-mold schools.

Edison.   Edison was only the second major profit-seeking U.S. venture to propose to operate public schools on an outsourced basis—and it immediately encountered resistance, both to the profit motive and to the loss of establishment control that is a byproduct of outsourcing. Although "reinventing government" by introducing private-sector competition into the delivery of public services was gaining traction in other sectors, K–12 education was slow to embrace this concept.

Outsourcing was not the original game plan. Chris Whittle's Edison Project was conceived in the early 1990s—around the same time as NAS—as a chain of futuristic private schools, precisely because Whittle understood the difficulty of making fundamental change within public education. But just as he and his colleagues were concluding that the economics of their grand private school plan did not add up, two promising innovations arose within public education, which Edison pivoted to take advantage of: the debut (thanks to Educational Alternatives, Inc.) of outsourcing entire schools to private operators, and the emergence of charter schools more or less outside the system. That pivot, however, meant that the rules, norms, politics, and budgets of public education rather than private markets would thereafter determine the venture's fate. One thing led to another, and here is how the (renamed) company describes itself today:

> EdisonLearning works with educators and communities to improve public schools and boost student performance. Our expertise and the value we bring to clients results from over 17 years experience not only servicing but operating public schools in collaboration with districts, boards, and other authorities with whom we partner.[8]

Edison was handicapped by the sorry precedent set by E.A.I., which failed in both Baltimore and Hartford, while sensitizing the public education establishment to the threat of outsourcing and setting that establishment's teeth on edge with regard to profiteering.

Disingenuousness abounds in this area, for public education has long purchased all manner of goods and services from profit-making firms that range from transportation companies to food-service suppliers to the purveyors of computers, textbooks, and even pencils and paper. Profitable activity is widespread in the instructional area, too, as many school systems outsource their Title I programs to private tutoring firms or contract with outside organizations for special education services. Yet E.A.I., then Edison, and subsequently all manner of other profit-seeking entities (including K12) ran into heavy fire when they proposed to make a profit by operating entire schools and furnishing their whole instructional program.

While Edison's relatively low-tech school design had merit—not so much a mold-breaker as a coherent pulling together of many promising practices and good ideas—this project, too, swiftly found itself with government as essentially its only customer, as well as its regulator and competitor. Inevitably, that situation led to dilution and compromise of the school design and major implementation challenges, particularly with respect to funding, personnel, and the myriad compliance and accountability obligations of both district-operated and charter public schools, not to mention shifting policy priorities and unstable election results.

Although it had a single, coherent school design, Edison never quite cracked the replication nut. Some of its schools succeeded admirably, while others (including some in Philadelphia) were dismal. Often the reason was personnel: Did they pick the right leader for a particular school? Was such a person available in that locale? More often, however, Edison's promising model was undermined by the local compromises that were demanded of it. Furthermore, state standards, tests, and accountability systems turn out to differ enough to pose a significant challenge to any would-be national template for curriculum and instruction.[9] And the objections to profiting from public schooling never abated. Particularly since personnel, mostly teachers, are the main budget item of every school, the obvious way to squeeze some profit from the same revenue is to employ fewer of them or pay them less. This was certain to be unpopular with the unions. When Edison's test results were not good enough, the inevitable response was, "You should take that money you are making for your investors and spend it on the kids instead."

It is no wonder that Edison began to search for less contentious lines of work—and, like Microsoft, also sought other countries in which to work.

K12 Inc. K12 had a better profitability plan. It would not need as many teachers because most instruction would be delivered online, and it would not need school buildings or building maintenance because most instruction would take place in students' homes or other nonschool settings. Yet the company faced huge up-front capital needs in acquiring all its technology and developing interactive online courses, tutorials, assessments, and management systems.

K12 faced other challenges, too. Insofar as the firm sought to sell its program directly to homeschooling parents via the private market, it encountered competitors and price sensitivity. And when it sought to establish virtual charter schools, it ran up against a host of difficulties with the public sector and the education establishment, of which objections to the profit motive were just the beginning. These problems included:

- How to price its product, considering that states paid varying amounts per pupil to their charter schools. Why should the same identical education program charge more in high-spending Massachusetts than the sums it apparently found sufficient in low-spending California? How could an online program justify charging as much as brick-and-mortar schools when its facility and personnel costs were obviously lower?
- A shelf of varied but irksome, sometimes crippling, state-specific constraints on charter schooling in general and on "virtual" schooling in particular. Some charter laws restricted enrollment to children living in a particular location, which made little sense when instruction was being delivered through the Internet and could as easily reach youngsters in Stockholm or Bangkok. Some states insisted on a maximum pupil-teacher ratio, even though K12 was engaged in distance learning via, for the most part, prepackaged lessons rather than real-time interaction between students and instructors.
- A boatload of competitors—some excellent, some shoddy, both national and local.
- Diverse state standards and assessments—which all had to be "aligned" with a national curriculum.
- Implementation woes, some peculiar to the virtual-instruction model. Is there enough bandwidth in people's homes? Who shoulders the risk when providing students with company-purchased computers? Other questions arose from the fact that the program was not exclusively online. For example, each K12 pupil was to receive at home a carton of physical materials—manipulatives, science equipment, traditional books, and such—but getting these delivered on schedule to thousands of different addresses posed a daunting logistical challenge.
- Market limits. How many families really have the desire and capacity to educate their children at home even if someone else is furnishing the instruction?

- Public (and parental) anxiety about virtual schooling's inability to deliver such nonacademic desiderata as sports and socialization.
- Unexpected resistance within the homeschooling community itself, some of whose leaders are so government phobic that they reject the charter school idea even when nearly all the teaching and learning takes place under parental supervision.

When Bill Bennett, Lowell Milken, and a few other deep-pocketed investors launched K12 in 1999, it was with the expectations, first, that America's growing population of homeschoolers—wielding their own checkbooks and credit cards—would eagerly purchase a high-quality, technology-based, curriculum-and-instruction program; and, second, that the fast-growing charter world would eagerly embrace virtual schooling.

The company is still doing both those things with some success, but it, too, increasingly wants to partner with traditional districts and sell its products as curriculum supplements to regular public schools. Its Web site now describes three main channels by which "tens of thousands of students" are helped to achieve "their true personal possibility":

- Full-time online public schools in many states across the country
- Individual course and product sales directly to families
- A growing number of public schools across the country, which are engaged in bringing individualized learning approaches into the traditional classroom

In other words, K12, like Edison and NAS before it, is finding that the regular old school system is now its principal client and inescapable rule-maker.

TECHNOLOGY AND THE LIMITS OF SCHOOL REFORM

SOF has avoided many of the tribulations of K12, Edison, and NAS. It is not trying to make a profit, at least not here and now. It does not educate kids at home. It operates in just one place so does not have to deal with varying academic standards and dissimilar testing and accountability systems. It is not a charter school, nor does it do true outsourcing. Its educators are covered by Philadelphia's union contract. It turns out, however, to share one specific liability with these other ventures: personnel, especially in the principal's office. More important, it shares the larger challenge of having to work with—indeed, within—public education and all that this means. It also lacks the organizational insulation—mainly via charter laws and outsourcing contracts—that Edison and K12 typically enjoyed. It does not have dependable continuity mechanisms, at least not the formal kind. (Its informal equivalents have served it well.) And being a small one-off, it does not have the weight of high-profile national ventures (although, again, it has had a more-than-serviceable substitute in the form of Microsoft's corporate involvement).

Like NAS, Edison, and K12, SOF benefits from a rich stock of extra resources, experts, advocates, rainmakers, and political protectors—but that advantage poses its own challenge for anyone thinking of scaling such an innovation. Even if the prototype succeeds, can such additional assets realistically be marshaled in quantity and sustained over time? To be sure, the "unit cost" declines as the model is field-tested, improved, and replicated, but creating new schools never achieves the economies of scale or predictability of, say, building Hampton Inns or opening Chipotle franchises. And as long as the school model deviates from the district norm, it will need yet more special resources to launch and keep going.

With the rarest of exceptions—and almost never in K–12 education—America's public sector is ill equipped to provide such venture capital and targeted assistance. Its mechanisms favor sameness and equity, not originality and uniqueness. That is why private-sector investment and involvement have proven critical to innovation in primary-secondary schooling—but also why the public sector into which they intrude is seldom welcoming or helpful. This, of course, causes the private entrepreneurs to tiptoe, ingratiate themselves, and not make needless waves. This in turn limits their capacity—and eventually even their ardor—to effect major reforms. For the flow of private capital to continue, acceptable profit margins must be visible. But for that to happen, the capitalists must not alienate their customers.

Today, both K12 and Edison—neither of which proved securely profitable or easily scalable with its original format—are putting themselves forward more as vendors of curriculum and instruction to other people's schools than as school operators (although they still do that, too). They have concluded, probably correctly, that (a) the market is vastly larger if you supply existing schools than if you try to launch or take over your own; and (b) the hassles and push back are far less, particularly for for-profit firms, because U.S. school systems are accustomed to buying curricular materials, professional development, and technical assistance from such companies. They have also deduced that (c) the potential profit margins are wider (and easier to justify politically); and (d) they will not be directly accountable for school results in the fraught NCLB era or held responsible for the million pain-in-the-rear issues (parental satisfaction, pupil discipline, human resource challenges) that arise when one is actually running schools.

One might even say that Edison and K12 are coming around to the Microsoft (and eventual NAS design-team) approach, functioning as suppliers, consultants, cheerleaders, troubleshooters, advisors, and mentors, rather than as school operators. In other words, they are now doing things for which one tends to get thanked and paid by the public education establishment rather than criticized, picketed, and sued.

But, of course, there is a profound trade-off. Vendors are not reformers. Consultants are not agitators. In real political cycles (and the lives of real kids), ventures that opt—or are forced—to work with and within the system are not going to transform it overnight, not going to compete with it, not going to provide alternatives to it, and not going to do anything that angers it.

Technology itself has boundless potential in education, as Clayton Christensen, John Chubb, and Terry Moe have recently noted (and as Lewis Perelman presciently pointed out in 1992).[10] The sky is the limit in terms of what it *could* do to strengthen instruction, foster learning, and boost productivity—not to mention all the back-office, managerial, and communications gains that might also be made with its help. The limiting factors on its use in K–12 education are not inherent in the technology itself (with minor, manageable exceptions, such as electrical capacity and bandwidth). Rather, what limits technology are the same factors that limit nontechnological innovations and reforms, including heterodox teacher-compensation plans, school calendars, accountability schemes, and choice programs.

Here is the paradox: the best way to deal with the political and regulatory obstacles—if one is bent on reforming education rather than simply making a buck from it—is to circumnavigate them by starting and running one's own schools as independently as possible. That means operating outside or semi-outside the system, via outsourcing or chartering, as both Edison and K12 set out to do; winning exemptions from constraints; getting waivers from rules; sidestepping collective bargaining agreements; and generally poking holes through at least some of the limitations.

Yet starting and running one's own schools, whether innovative or not, tech-heavy or not, brings a boatload of other problems, all manner of push backs and constraints—and a great deal of vulnerability to changing circumstances, people, and priorities in the policy sphere. The system and its unstable collection of fickle political overlords and unchanging bureaucratic procedures continue to set the rules by which exceptions are encouraged, tolerated, and contained—and in K–12 education, those rules are far more elaborate than in, say, postsecondary or preschool education.

To avoid those vulnerabilities while enlarging their markets faster than such exceptions can ever grow, the developers and promoters of technological innovation in education prudently—or despairingly—steer away from full-fledged school operations (or, in Microsoft's case, never enter into it) and instead opt to become vendors of curriculum, instruction, software, and expertise to the system itself. But that is a Faustian bargain, too. For now the system becomes their customer—very likely their primary, if not sole, customer—and its constraints and norms, its needs and practices, take over. Vendors wanting to keep doing business with the system have little choice but to accommodate its wants and limits, its procedures and timelines, its idiosyncrasies, and folkways. This brings us nearly full circle: either one works in those ways with the system, in which case one does not do much reforming; or one works from outside to create alternative options, in which case the system delimits how much one can actually do.

By happenstance, both Edison and K12 also learned those painful lessons in Philadelphia in the post-Vallas era. He had outsourced some thirty low-performing district schools to Edison (and a dozen more to other for-profit and nonprofit operators) as part of his effort to transform the school system's academic results, as well as its organizational structure. He also entered into contracts with K12 to advise the district on science curriculum and to take charge of science instruction in one middle school.

But, for reasons that had more to do with politics (and race relations) than educational effectiveness, K12's Philadelphia contracts were terminated or not renewed.[11] Edison is still there, managing fewer schools, delivering mixed results—and rather chastened by the experience. The company learned the hard way that the adjustments it agreed to make in its model (particularly with regard to personnel selection and management) truly did impair its capacity to run successful schools. It also learned that a working relationship that was cordial enough while Vallas ran the show was destined to become more acrimonious when the revolving door spun.

Philadelphia illustrates the big, ugly reality that America's established public education system is nearly impregnable to changes, interruptions, innovations, and challenges that it does not want. Although its wants appear to fluctuate in quixotic ways, its true pace of change is glacial and, of course, its performance can charitably be described as uneven to unsatisfactory, especially for poor kids in urban communities. Yet it is awesomely well fortified to resist assault, save where it sees the invader as bringing something that can be turned to the system's own benefit—and even then the entrepreneur may be out on his ear a year or two later when the system's theories or priorities revolve again.

Thus, the system has largely succeeded in tempering the changes sought by promoters of standards, assessments, and results-based accountability (particularly forms of accountability that might affect adults employed by the system). Never mind that the "outsiders" advancing these changes are usually governors, legislators, and influential tycoons.

Where the system has yielded to such reforms, it has usually been because extra money was also offered, whether from the public purse, private philanthropy, or venture capitalists. Yet even then the changes typically last through just one or two election cycles before the K–12 enterprise snaps back into something resembling its previous configuration, like a rubber band that allowed itself to be stretched but never stopped yearning to resume its original shape.

The public education system has also succeeded, for the most part, in fending off, containing, co-opting, or slowly vanquishing the changes sought by advocates of choice-based reforms, such as charter schools and vouchers. (Although millions of young Americans now attend schools that their parents choose, the overwhelming majority of those schools are themselves creatures of the system—and not so different from the rest of the system.)

Even so potent and dynamic a force as technological change has come slowly and painfully to K–12 education, which is notably less altered by modern telecommunications, the Internet, and the cyber revolution than most other realms of contemporary life. Indeed, as Tom Vander Ark recently wrote, "Education remains one of the few sectors that information and communication technologies have not transformed."[12] Although the kids themselves are consumed by such developments, that is mostly outside of school. (Observe how many schools ban cell phones, text messaging, and such on their premises; how many teachers lack their own laptops, e-mail access, even at-work phone numbers; and how often computers are still confined to special labs or isolated in the back of the classroom.) Public education generally views technology as a supplement or special program for which—once again—additional money must be found, not as a powerful productivity enhancer or cost-effective substitute for traditional personnel.

The organizational structure and management culture of American public education are not well adapted to the information age, so we ought not be surprised by technology's awkward fit within the K–12 enterprise.

The distinguished technology historian Thomas P. Hughes might well have been describing U.S. school systems when he wrote:

> Hierarchy, specialization, standardization, centralization, expertise, and bureaucracy became the hallmarks of management during the second industrial revolution. [But] flatness, interdisciplinarity, heterogeneity, distributed control, meritocracy, and nimble flexibility characterize information-age management.[13]

To date, therefore, the main value of SOF to the K–12 enterprise is approximately what Microsoft intended it to be: a demonstration site where, as Kant said, the actual proves the possible. It shows that technology can do a lot more for education than the system normally allows it to.

That is worth demonstrating, yet it is no real surprise. Indeed, it is much the same conclusion that Microsoft reached when it determined from the SOF experience that technology itself is not the source of the vexing constraints on its own transformative potential in the public education sphere. Rather, the SOF tale illustrates the stop-and-go, three-inches-forward, two-inches-back nature of change in American public education. This sector is not permanently immune to developments in the world around it or to shifting needs and demands on the part of its clients, funders, and elected officials.[14] But it seldom behaves in the ways that outside innovators and entrepreneurs favor, and it never operates on their timetable. Most important—and frustrating—is that the system that needs to change remains largely in control of the change process and can thus dictate terms to those innovators and entrepreneurs, or else tame them into accepting its terms as a more prudent and potentially more rewarding path than competing with or harassing it.

10

The Value of Transparency, Not Just Evaluation

Frederick M. Hess and Mary Cullinane

IN THE PREVIOUS CHAPTER, Chester E. Finn drew on his wealth of experience and knowledge to put SOF in historical context while distilling and making sense of two decades worth of lessons in the realm of school redesign and technology-based improvement. Rather than reiterate Finn's insights, we want just to share some closing thoughts, primarily on the creation and implementation of SOF and the importance of transparency in school improvement.

America's public schools are supposed to be just that, *public* schools. Yet community members, parents, and researchers too often find it difficult to get a close look at schools and school systems. As a result, the very public that public schools exist to serve can feel alienated from local education systems. This careful analysis of SOF marks a substantial effort to illuminate the inner workings of one high-profile effort at high school redesign. By inviting a team of researchers, SOF, Microsoft, and the School District of Philadelphia showed a commitment to its various constituents and stakeholders. Not only does this exercise do a service to students and community members in Philadelphia, it provides valuable examples for urban reformers across the land.

Because this kind of close scrutiny is so rare, important and obvious lessons can be overlooked or remain unacknowledged. School of the Future represents a dramatic effort to launch a new school within the confines of a district. It represents a bet that it is possible to redesign a high school within the framework of district managerial, accountability, and personnel systems. The challenges that SOF has faced in doing so, even as it started with a fresh slate in a new building and with substantial external support, help to illustrate how hard it can be to build coherent new organizations in urban districts. That experience holds important lessons for today's proponents of school "turnarounds," as federal officials and leading philanthropists are urging districts to transform troubled schools by replacing school leadership and staff. The SOF experience shows that such efforts are anything but self-executing, and that the challenges of establishing a new curriculum and a sturdy school culture cannot be lightly wished away.

More generally, the SOF experience reminds us of five crucial lessons for high school reform, and for technology-assisted reform more generally. The first is that the story was never about the program, the design, or the toys, but about the people who made it work. At School of the Future, as in so many district schools and charter schools, it proved enormously difficult for faculty to know how to operate in this new school. The second is that leadership instability, outside of the school as well as in the school, made it more difficult to establish a clear and consistent curriculum or culture. The third is that it became increasingly difficult, as SOF's original champions moved on or took new positions, to maintain the arrangements that were supposed to give SOF the autonomy it needed to thrive. The fourth is that the SOF experience shows that contemporary notions of instructional leadership too often shortchange the reality that—at least in tumultuous districts—school leaders need to be politically savvy advocates for their schools who are able to "manage up," and not simply instructional leaders who can "manage down." And, finally, the greatest challenge SOF faced was its infancy. Without having the time to build a culture strong enough to weather the significant challenges of urban education, the challenges SOF faced proved overwhelming at times. The fact that SOF has survived through this period of infancy and continues to work toward its goals demonstrates the strength of its convictions and developmental process. We must find better ways to protect organizations in their early years, especially those whose mission and practice are in tension with the status quo. Without these protections, many will fail.

Amid all of the frustrations and challenges, however, the faculty of SOF also remind us that many a green shoot can be spotted at SOF. And this is an important reminder. When we focus only on test scores and see that school A or program B is doing well, we too often imagine that they're doing everything right. And if we bother to look at the messy reality of a new venture and see all the frustrations and uncertainties, we often imagine that it will never work. Both tendencies reflect a desire to shrink from the frustrating realities of the real world. Many heralded schools and school systems start to look much less lovely up close, and most splendid efforts have had their share of stumbles and frustrations. The key is to learn from them and to use them wisely.

A rigorous examination of SOF shows the granular impact of important design decisions. By opting to make SOF a regular district school, its founders consciously adopted a course that would impose staffing constraints, shape the student body, and leave the school subject to district politics and leadership turnover. Decisions regarding curriculum created complications that also required additional time and energy for staff. Understanding the significance of these stumbling blocks is not a question of evaluation focused on test results but of looking into routines, culture, and organizational practice.

Indeed, there is often a "heads I win, tails you lose" dynamic to transparency. In places where test results are compelling, allowing researchers to dig around and unearth haphazard or questionable practices offers no benefits. When scores are high and public acclaim has followed, closer scrutiny can only tarnish a district's image. If test results are not impressive, even compelling evidence that a school or district is well managed will be met with a shrug or disbelief. In short, there is little incentive for anyone to invite the kind of careful scrutiny that can broadly inform those looking for lessons about what they should and should not do.

Essential to promoting transparency is the process of encouraging outsiders to see how things work, to float alternative perspectives, and to bring a fresh pair of eyes. This kind of introspection constitutes, in fact, both the first and final I's in Microsoft's 6I Development Process—a discipline that is all too rare in a sector where reformers have a tendency to leap from one bandwagon to the next without paying much heed to why or how popular strategies actually work. Of course, the value of understanding how the sausage is actually made conflicts with the old adage that you never want to see sausage or legislation being made as you risk losing your appetite for both.

For transparency to pay off, it is vital that we not shrink from the messy truth of the sausage factory. Unfortunately, our tendency is just the opposite. Reporters and writers typically identify "successful" or "high-flying" schools and then write sentimental, heroic accounts that lionize the educators in question while whitewashing most of the practical challenges. This tradition fosters a notion that messy organizational travails are simple predictors of performance, thus creating a culture in which organizations are rewarded for hiding the messy challenges of launching or expanding. One consequence is that anyone who spends much time around charter schooling or education's "new sector" will not infrequently have the disconcerting sensation of seeing organizations praised for their management acumen when one knows, behind the screen, that those organizations are paragons of disorder.

The run-up to this volume featured a disheartening but not uncommon illustration of the kind of journalism and popular reaction that tends to stifle inquiry and discourage schools and districts from welcoming helpful scrutiny. In May 2009, the first drafts of the research in this volume were presented at a conference in Washington, D.C., hosted by the American Enterprise Institute. The intent was to foster debate, invite criticism, and share findings with the policy community. Despite repeated reminders by the conference chair that this was a formative rather than a summative assessment, one reporter seized on the discussion as an opportunity to attack SOF and embarrass Microsoft.

In an article headlined "School of the Future: Lessons in Failure," a reporter for the leading industry newspaper *eSchool News* wrote, "Three years, three superintendents, four principals, and countless problems later, experts at . . . the American Enterprise Institute (AEI) agreed: The Microsoft-inspired project has been a failure so far."[1] Not only did this mischaracterize the findings and discussion, which were explicitly billed as formative rather than evaluative, but it brushed past the rare opportunity to look inside the "black box" of school design. In fact, as contributor Matthew Riggan noted in an eloquent response to *eSchool News*:

> Both the authors and conference conveners went to considerable lengths to note that these studies were not intended to be evaluative, yet from its very title . . . [the] article reports their findings as if they were. This misrepresents the research, but more importantly it does a disservice to those teachers, principals, and students who shared their experiences with us and were extraordinarily candid about their struggles.[2]

Indeed, if we are to encourage smart, honest discourse about how to use technology effectively in schooling or make redesign work at scale, we will need far more looking behind the curtain and far less casual celebration of schools or districts that remain largely free from the limelight.

As Harvard education professor Chris Dede has wryly observed, "This [kind of coverage] is consistent with my long experience trying to discuss educational technologies with the media. They love to portray technology as magic, then debunk it as useless. Both sell papers, whereas nuanced discourse does not."[3] Even though the editor of *eSchool News*, Greg Downey, released a subsequent commentary stating his regrets for elements of the earlier piece, including the perception of failure caused by the headline, the damage was done. Such statements of regret are never heard as loudly as the message that caused the reaction.[4] It can only be hoped that reformers, educators, and foundations will increasingly promote such a culture and reward those schools, districts, and providers that invite scrutiny—thus countering the incentives that may lead some partisans or sensation-seeking journalists to penalize openness.

In the end, school redesign is an opportunity rather than a guarantee. Despite enthusiastic supporters who seek to wish away the political and institutional hurdles of school improvement, technology is a tool and is only as useful as the hand that wields it. This is a lesson that is too frequently forgotten, whether the issue is linking schools to the Web, distance education, or laptop computer programs. As David Dwyer, an education professor at Stanford University, has observed:

> Technology is only the vehicle we may ride as we work to engage more children in the excitement and life-enhancing experience of learning. We will drive along a road that is paved by our public, collective will to build a modern, equitable, effective education system. Will it be a superhighway? Or a bumpy road of cobblestones—outmoded teaching strategies, low standards, out-of-date texts, limited assessment systems, and overburdened agendas?[5]

These are the questions we have too rarely confronted, even while investing technology with grand hopes and aspirations. Indeed, school improvement is arduous, controversial, and sometimes frustrating work. Change takes time, commitment, and seriousness. Producing sustainable changes in attitudes, behavior, and expectations is not the work of a season or a year, and all innovations must survive early stumbles. Improving instruction, strengthening content, using technology wisely, and building dynamic management and support systems is challenging, especially where school systems have too long languished amid instability and incoherence. Urban reform efforts are unlikely to succeed among the kind of unstable leadership, inchoate governance, and desire for silver-bullet reforms that have characterized urban public education systems for more than a generation.

Our hope is that the kind of transparent, public, systematic inquiry embodied by this volume will help inspire similar efforts elsewhere. We believe that this kind of endeavor provides an opportunity for realistic self-assessment, can serve as an antidote to the overwrought claims of reformers and their critics, can permit reform efforts to be parsed in a more thoughtful and insightful manner, and can offer an opportunity for the national community of educators and would-be reformers to learn from one another's experiences—both from those that prove successful and those that are more frustrating.

In the end, with or without technology, meaningful school redesign is about incentives, policies, organizations, politics, and people—all the same frustrating stumbling blocks that have so often impeded grand new designs. School redesign is an opportunity to do things better and smarter, but it takes time and patience and will only be as effective as how well it is implemented. Similarly, even wondrous technology will not deliver if it is offered as a self-executing panacea, or if it is imagined as a deus ex machina that will transform our schools and classrooms despite the human element. SOF demonstrates that even in circumstances where these cautions are recognized, the challenges of the twenty-first century are daunting and should not be underestimated. Practitioners, policymakers, and stakeholders alike will have to learn from both our successes and our mistakes, pay due heed to the gritty details of implementation and execution, and recognize that there are no shortcuts to excellence.

Notes

Chapter 1

1. Clayton M. Christensen, Michael B. Horn, and Custis Johnson, *Disrupting Class: How Disruptive Innovation Will Change the Way the World Learns* (New York: McGraw Hill, 2009).

2. Terry M. Moe and John E. Chubb, *Liberating Learning: Technology, Politics, and the Future of American Education* (San Francisco: Wiley, 2009), 7, 150.

3. Todd Oppenheimer, *The Flickering Mind: The False Promise of Technology in the Classroom and How Learning Can Be Saved* (New York: Random House, 2003), 393.

4. Mark Dynarski et al., "Effectiveness of Reading and Mathematics Software: Finding from the First Student Cohort" (Washington, DC: U.S. Department of Education, 2007), http://ies.ed.gov/ncee/pubs/20074005/.

5. Katie McMillan Culp, Margaret Honey, and Ellen Mandinach, *A Retrospective on Twenty Years of Education Technology Policy* (Washington, DC: U.S. Department of Education, 2003), http://www.ed.gov/rschstat/eval/tech/20years.pdf, 21, 22.

6. Charles Fisher, David C. Dwyer, and Keith Yocam, eds., *Education and Technology* (San Francisco: Jossey-Bass, 1996), 1–7.

7. Decker F. Walker, "Toward an ACOT of Tomorrow," in *Education and Technology*, eds. Charles Fisher, David C. Dwyer, and Keith Yocam (San Francisco: Jossey-Bass, 1996), 98.

8. Jan Hawkins, "Dilemmas," in *Education and Technology* (see note 7), 38.

9. Brent R. Keltner, *Funding Comprehensive School Reform* (Santa Monica, CA: RAND Corporation, 1998).

10. Elizabeth Hertling, "Implementing Whole-School Reform," *ERIC Digests* (2004), http://www.ericdigests.org/2002-1/reform.html.

11. Jim McChesney, "Whole-School Reform," *ERIC Digests* (1998), http://www.ericdigests.org/1999-4/reform.htm.

12. Ibid.

13 Thomas K. Glennan Jr., *New American Schools after Six Years* (Santa Monica, CA: RAND Corporation, 1998).

14. American Institutes for Research, *An Educator's Guide to Schoolwide Reform* (Arlington, VA: Educational Research Service, 1999).

15. New American Schools, *Working Toward Excellence: Results from Schools Implementing New American Schools Designs* (Richmond, TX: New American Schools, 1999), www.naschools.org/resource/earlyind/99Results.pdf.

16. Thomas Toch, *High Schools on a Human Scale: How Small Schools Can Transform American Education* (Boston: Beacon Press, 2003).

17. Linda Shaw, "Foundation's Small School Experiment Has Yet to Yield Big Results," *Seattle Times*, November 5, 2006, http://seattletimes.nwsource.com/html/localnews/2003348701_gates05m.html.

18. Barbara Schneider, Adam Wyse, and Venessa Keesler, "Is Small Really Better? Testing Some Assumptions about High School Size," *Brookings Papers on Education Policy: 2006–2007*, eds. Tom Loveless and Frederick M. Hess (Washington, DC: Brookings Institution Press, 2007).

19. Valerie Lee and Julia Smith, "High School Size: Which Works Best and for Whom?" *Educational Evaluation and Policy Analysis* 19, no. 3 (1997): 205–227.

20. Caroline Hoxby, "The Effects of Class Size on Student Achievement: New Evidence from Population Variation," *Quarterly Journal of Economics* 115, no. 4 (2000).

21. David D. Marsh and Judy B. Codding, "The New American High School" (Thousand Oaks, CA: Corwin Press, 1998), 139–140.

22. High Tech High Foundation, "High Tech High—About High Tech High," http://www.hightechhigh.org/about/.

23. High Tech High Foundation, "High Tech High—HTH Facilities," http://www.hightechhigh.org/about/facilities.php.

24. "About High Tech High School" (information page on Hudson County Schools of Technology website), http://www1.hcstonline.org/hths/.

25. New Technology Foundation, "New Technology Foundation," http://www. newtechfoundation.org.

26. New Technology Foundation, "New Technology Foundation—About Us," http://www.newtechfoundation.org/about.html.

27. New Technology Foundation, "New Technology Foundation—Partnerships," http://www.newtechfoundation.org/about_partnerships.html.

28. Victor Asal and Paul Hardwood, *Educating the First Digital Generation: Educate Us* (Westport, CT: Praeger, 2007); Lesley Farmer, *Teen Girls and Technology: What's the Problem, What's the Solution?* (New York: Teacher's College Press, 2008).

29. David Kritt and Lucian Winegar, eds., *Education and Technology: Critical Perspectives, Possible Futures* (Lanham, MD: Lexington Books, 2007); Marge Cambre and Mark Hawkes, *Toys, Tools & Teachers: The Challenges of Technology* (Lanham, MD: Rowman & Littlefield, 2004).

30. Andrew Zucker, *Transforming Schools with Technology* (Cambridge, MA: Harvard Education Press, 2008); Mary Burns and K. Victoria Dimock, *Technology as a Catalyst for School Communities: Beyond Boxes and Bandwidth* (Lanham, MD: Rowman & Littlefield, 2007); Eileen Coppola, *Powering Up: Learning to Teach Well with Technology* (New York: Teacher's College Press, 2004).

31. Walker, "Toward an ACOT of Tomorrow," 103.

32. Hawkins, "Dilemmas," 49.

33. Jane L. David, "Developing and Spreading Accomplished Teaching: Policy Lessons from a Unique Partnership," in *Education and Technology* (see note 7), 238.

34. The students, educators, and administrators interviewed for this volume were selected by the school or self-selected, and therefore they comprise a small and decidedly nonrandom sample—it is difficult to know how representative their experiences and insights are.

Chapter 2
1. Being LEED certified means they have passed standards set by the U.S. Green Building Council for environmentally sustainable construction. Gold is their ranking (rankings are basic, silver, gold, and platinum).

2. The Loop process requires that many individuals interview each candidate. They must ask consistent questions and record candidates' responses and their reactions to the responses. The process, although time consuming, is intended to be thorough and objective. Information about the Competency Wheel and the entire Loop process is documented on the Microsoft Education Web site and is available for any organization to adapt and use freely. The Competency Wheel was to become part of the human resources process in the district to improve the selection and hiring of high-quality teachers for all schools in the district.

Chapter 4

1. Phillip Hallinger and Ronald H. Heck, "Exploring the Principal's Contribution to School Effectiveness: 1980–1995," *School Effectiveness and School Improvement* 9, no. 2 (1998): 157–191; Kenneth Leithwood, *Educational Leadership: A Review of the Research* (Philadelphia: Mid-Atlantic Regional Educational Laboratory, 2005).

2. Mark Berends, Susan Bodilly, and Sheila Nataraj Kirby, "New American Schools: District and School Leadership for Whole-School Reform," in *Leadership Lessons from Comprehensive School Reforms*, eds. Joseph Murphy and Amanda Datnow (Thousand Oaks, CA: Corwin Press, 2004), 109–131.

3. James P. Spillane, Richard Halverson, and John Diamond, "Towards a Theory of School Leadership Practice: Implications of a Distributed Perspective," *Journal of Curriculum Studies* 36 (2004): 3–34; Peter Gronn, "Distributed Leadership," in the *Second International Handbook of Educational Leadership and Administration*, eds. Kenneth Leithwood and Karen Seashore-Louis (Dordrecht, Netherlands: Kluwer, 2002), 653–696.

4. Microsoft Corporation, *Building the School of the Future*, Discovery Brief 04: Strategic Leadership Selection (Redmond, WA: Microsoft Corporation, 2006), 4.

5. Council of Chief State School Officers, *Educational Leadership Policy Standards: ISLLC 2008* (Washington, DC: Council of Chief State School Officers, 2008).

6. Robert W. Echinger and Michael M. Lombardo, *Professional Leadership: Education Competency Wheel* (Minneapolis: Lominger Limited, 2003).

7. Ibid.

8. Microsoft, *Building the School of the Future*, 1.

9. Microsoft, *Building the School of the Future*.

10. Kate Hayes and Mary Cullinane, "School of the Future: 2007 Community Reflection and Review" (presentation to the School District of Philadelphia, 2007).

11. University Council for Education Administration, *The Revolving Door of the Principalship* (Austin, TX: University Council for Educational Administration, 2008).

12. Bruce Buchanan, *Turnover at the Top: Superintendent Vacancies and the Urban School* (Blue Ridge Summit, PA: Rowman and Littlefield, 2006).

13. Henry M. Levin, "Why Is This So Difficult?" in *Educational Entrepreneurship: Realities, Challenges, Possibilities,* ed. Frederick M. Hess (Cambridge, MA: Harvard Education Press, 2006), 165–182.

Chapter 5

1. Donna Penn Towns, Beverly Cole-Henderson, and Zewelanji Serpell, "The Journey to Urban School Success: Going the Extra Mile," *Journal of Negro Education* 70, no. 1 (2001): 4–18.

2. See, for example, Peter Scales, Eugene Roehlkepartain, Neal Marybeth, James Kielsmeir, and Peter Benson, "Reducing Academic Achievement Gaps: The Role of Community Service and Service Learning," *Journal of Experiential Education* 29, no. 1 (2006): 38–60. This study found that "principals in high-poverty, urban, and majority nonwhite schools were more likely to judge service-learning's impact on student attendance, engagement, and academic achievement as very positive. Students with higher levels of service/service-learning reported higher grades, attendance, and other academic success outcomes. Low-SES students with service/service-learning scored better on most academic success variables than their low-SES peers with less or no service or service-learning."

3. Patrick McGuinn, "The Policy Landscape," in *Educational Entrepreneurship: Realities, Challenges, Possibilities,* ed. Frederick M. Hess (Cambridge, MA: Harvard Education Press, 2006).

4. Microsoft, School of the Future fact sheet, December 2008, http://www.microsoft.com/presspass/events/sof/docs/SOTFFS.doc.

5. Susan Eaton, *The Children in Room E4: American Education on Trial* (New York: Algonquin Books, 2007); Jean Anyon, *Ghetto Schooling: A Political Economy of Urban Educational Reform* (New York: Teachers College Press, 1997).

6. Terry Moe and John Chubb, *Liberating Learning: Technology, Politics, and the Future of American Education* (San Francisco: Jossey-Bass, 2009).

7. One administrator estimated that one-third of the SOF faculty are experienced, one-third are newly certified teachers from education schools, and one-third are career changers new to teaching.

8. Drexel University and the University of Pennsylvania were originally involved with SOF as well; although these partnerships have not been sustained, Drexel continues to house the SOF network servers.

9. "Urban School Superintendents: Characteristics, Tenure, and Salary," *Urban Indicator* 5, no. 2 (2000).

10. Joe Williams, "Entrepreneurs within School Districts," in *Educational Entrepreneurship: Realities* (see note 3).

11. Robert Maranto and April Maranto, "Markets, Bureaucracies, and Clans: The Role of Organizational Culture," in *Educational Entrepreneurship: Realities, Challenges, Possibilities* (see note 3).

12. Anthony Bryk, Valerie Lee, and Peter Holland, *Catholic Schools and the Common Good* (Cambridge, MA: Harvard University Press, 1993); John Chubb and Terry Moe, *Politics, Markets, and America's Schools* (Washington, DC: Brookings Institution Press, 1990).

13. However, as noted in other chapters in this volume, teacher hiring at SOF will continue to be significantly constrained by the need to operate within the district's dysfunctional personnel system and collective bargaining stipulations.

Chapter 6

1. Dale Mezzacappa, "Teachers May Lose Say in Placement," *Philadelphia Inquirer*, June 10, 2004.

2. By 2009, eighty-eight schools had opted for full site selection.

3. See http://www.microsoft.com/education/competencies/successprofile_highschoolteacher.mspx.

4. In the 1970s, the School District of Philadelphia and the Philadelphia Federation of Teachers entered into a consent decree requiring that the faculty at every school be balanced racially according to a formula related to the overall numbers of African American teachers in the system at each school level, within certain parameters. This is now part of the PFT contract; see http://pa.aft.org/pft/

?action=article&articleid=ab976caf-20e7-4570-b5e9-6f5831fd1674. As a result, some vacancies are listed with "AA only" or "white only" designations. There are no requirements for teachers of other ethnicities.

5. Although Philadelphia has a contract with Teach For America, there are no people from that program at SOF, primarily because those teachers are limited to assignments in schools that have the most difficulty filling all their positions. But many of the young educators who were hired at SOF had similar backgrounds, in that they did not major in education but instead in heavy-duty fields like cognitive science, engineering, and biology. The difference is that these recruits had decided on teaching as a career. One woman said she deliberately avoided the Teach For America route because she felt that the compressed summer training was too short. "I knew that I wasn't ready immediately graduating from college to come in and be the teacher I wanted to be," she said. "I wanted to have time to think before I got into a classroom." She chose the University of Pennsylvania's accelerated ten-month graduate certification program, which, in fact, has produced at least four members of the SOF faculty.

6. Since the school started with just one grade and added a grade each year, it took four rounds to build the entire staff. While the hiring process has varied somewhat each year, due mostly to the turnover in leadership both at the school and the district level, it has largely remained true to this Microsoft process, based on competencies and the "Loop."

7. See http://www.ascd.org/publications/books/107018/chapters/Related_ASCD_Resources@_Understanding_by_Design.aspx.

8. See http://webgui.phila.k12.pa.us/uploads/dr/HY/drHYRgSvGohGA84W7vPFJw/Imagine-2014-Strategic-Plan.pdf.

Chapter 7

1. From a student project, gathered by Kate Hayes on February 15, 2008.

2. Q's project proposal, March 11, 2008.

3. Q's final reflection, June 15, 2008.

4. Q's final reflection, June 15, 2008.

5. Microsoft Education Competencies; see http://www.microsoft.com/education/competencies/comp_strategicagilityandinnovationmanagement.mspx.

6. Ibid.

Chapter 8

1. Congressional testimony of Mary Cullinane, February 2008, www.microsoft. com/education/matters/cullinane.mspx.

2. The curriculum summit was a gathering of education stakeholders from Philadelphia and other locales, who were brought together to begin discussions on how the school would develop and deliver its curriculum.

3. Congressional testimony of Mary Cullinane, February 2008, www.microsoft. com/education/matters/cullinane.mspx.

4. All blogs posted in this chapter were quoted from "The School of the Future WebLog," http://blogs.msdn.com/phillyhi/archive/2004/02/15/73210.aspx.

5. Thomas C. Reeves, *The Impact of Media and Technology in Schools* (Athens: University of Georgia, Bertelsmann Foundation, 1998).

6. Ibid.

7. James J. Heckman and Paul A. LaFontaine, *The Declining American High School Graduation Rate: Evidence, Sources, and Consequences* (Cambridge, MA: National Bureau of Economic Research, 2008).

Chapter 9

1. I cannot state with absolute certainty that nobody at Microsoft ever envisioned a "chain" of SOF clones within the United States, but if they did, they kept their aspirations quiet—and later changed their plan. Since SOF was—and remains— an expense item for the company, not a revenue producer, and since its basic set- up shows no prospect of becoming a revenue producer, I am inclined to take at face value the statements of SOF's Microsoft team that this was always intended as a beta site and showcase rather than the first of many.

2. Dale Mezzacappa, "The Vallas Effect," *Education Next* 8, no. 2 (Spring 2008), http://www.hoover.org/publications/ednext/16109997.html.

3. Lynn Olson, "District Making 'Transition' to Bigger Supply of Schools of Choice," *Education Week*, February 9, 2005, http://www.edweek.org/ew/articles/20 05/02/09/22phillyside.h24.html?qs=K12+Philadelphia+science.

4. Microsoft Education, "School of the Future: Explore the Process," http://www. Microsoft.com/Education/SchoolofFutureProcess.mspx; Microsoft Education, "Competency Wheel," http://download.Microsoft.com/download/3/4/7/ 3477e49d-315d-4ee7-a8ca-ff653a4455d6/Competency_Wheel.pdf; Microsoft

Education, "Overview," http://www.Microsoft.com/education/uspil/institute/overview.aspx.

5. Microsoft Education, "Innovative Schools Program Participating Members," http://www.Microsoft.com/education/pil/ISc_members.aspx. These "innovative schools" are not, however, without replication challenges of their own. A colleague who has spent time in the Brazil school reports that its "technology was not innovative at all there; kids used the free access to the Internet to play mindless games."

6. Jeffrey Mirel, *The Evolution of the New American Schools: From Revolution to Mainstream* (Washington, DC: Thomas B. Fordham Institute, 2001), http://www.edexcellence.net/doc/evolution.pdf.

7. Mark Berends, Susan J. Bodilly, and Sheila N. Kirby, *Facing the Challenges of Whole-School Reform: New American Schools after a Decade* (Santa Monica, CA: RAND Corporation, 2003).

8. From http://www.edisonlearning.com/about_us.

9. A little-discussed benefit of national standards and tests, if the United States ever gets there, is the simplification this will bring to all sorts of private vendors in the K–12 space—from school operators like Edison to textbook publishers like Pearson and Scholastic, which will no longer have to tailor their products to differing state standards. (The corresponding "losers" will be testing firms and test publishers, which benefit from today's cacophony.)

10. Clayton M. Christensen, Michael B. Horn, and Curtis W. Johnson, *Disrupting Class: How Disruptive Innovation Will Change the Way the World Learns* (New York: McGraw Hill, 2008); Terry M. Moe and John E. Chubb, *Liberating Learning: Technology, Politics, and the Future of American Education* (San Francisco: Jossey-Bass, 2009); Lewis J. Perelman, *School's Out: Hyperlearning, the New Technology, and the End of School* (New York: Avon Books, 1992).

11. Vallas's departure was not the whole story. K12 board chairman Bill Bennett had made some ill-advised race-related comments on his morning radio show—to which the African American community in Philadelphia (and Chicago) took strong exception. Vallas indicated to K12 that if Bennett remained in his position, the school system would no longer be able to work with the company. Bennett was dumped, and then Philadelphia dumped K12 anyway.

12. Tom Vander Ark, "Private Capital and Public Education: Toward Quality at Scale," working paper (Washington, DC: American Enterprise Institute, 2009).

13. Thomas P. Hughes, *Human-Built World: How to Think about Technology and Culture* (Chicago: University of Chicago Press, 2004).

14. David Tyack and Larry Cuban, *Tinkering Toward Utopia: A Century of Public School Reform* (Cambridge, MA: Harvard University Press, 1995).

Chapter 10

1. Meris Stansbury, "School of the Future: Lessons in Failure," *eSchool News*, June 1, 2009, http://www.eschoolnews.com/news/top-news/?i=58973.

2. Matthew Riggan, "Comment," *eSchool News*, June 3, 2009.

3. Personal communication from Chris Dede, June 3, 2009.

4. Greg Downey, "Editorial: Philadelphia Story. Transparency in Education Is a Rare Thing—Which Is Why Microsoft and AIE Are to Be Commended," *eSchool News*, July 3, 2009, http://www.eschoolnews.com/news/top-news/index.cfm?i=59545.

5. David C. Dwyer, "Education and Technology," in *Education and Technology*, eds. Charles Fisher, David C. Dwyer, and Keith Yocam (San Francisco: Jossey-Bass, 1996), 98.

Acknowledgments

IN 2003, MICROSOFT and the School District of Philadelphia agreed to form a partnership that would investigate, determine, and deliver a high school equipped to prepare learners for the twenty-first century. The goal was to build and redefine the norm for urban high school education. While technology would be a critical element, it would not define the school's mission. Since 2003, the challenges and victories of this work have yielded many lessons for the education community.

In an effort to highlight the teachable moments of this project, Microsoft sought the assistance of the American Enterprise Institute to identify critical outside observers who could provide perspectives on these challenges and victories. While School of the Future continues to be a work in progress, it is imperative that such school reform efforts be exposed to allow for authentic reflection. This volume is not a collection of conclusions, nor does it represent all perspectives. The ideas and reflections shared in this volume are a snapshot taken and considered with the hope of providing insight to others experiencing similar journeys.

We are deeply appreciative of everyone who contributed to or helped with the compilation of this volume. In particular, we thank the authors who wrote the conference drafts that were presented at the American Enterprise Institute in June 2009. We also thank the discussants who participated in that conference and gave invaluable feedback on those early papers. That stellar list of public officials, educators, and scholars included

Dennis Cheek, a senior fellow at the Ewing Marion Kauffman Foundation; Mitchell Chester, commissioner of the Massachusetts public schools; John Chubb, a distinguished visiting fellow at Stanford's Hoover Institution and senior executive vice president and cofounder of Edison Schools; Chris Dede, the Timothy E. Wirth Professor in Learning Technologies at Harvard's Graduate School of Education; Denis Doyle, the cofounder and chief academic officer of SchoolNet; Kate Hayes, a counselor at Philadelphia's School of the Future; Kent McGuire, dean of the College of Education and a professor in the Department of Educational Leadership and Policy Studies at Temple University; and Susan Schilling, CEO of the New Technology Foundation.

At the American Enterprise Institute, Thomas Gift did a sterling job of assembling, revising, and editing the papers for publication and assisting with the accompanying research and analysis. Raphael Gang, Morgan Goatley, Andrew Kelly, Rosemary Kendrick, Jenna Schuette, Juliet Squire, Greg Franke, and Ben Hyman also played critical roles in producing and editing the volume.

At the School District of Philadelphia and SOF, we wish to recognize the support of Dr. Arlene Ackerman, Mr. Tomas Hanna, Ms. Melanie Harris, Dr. Maria Pitre, and Mr. Bob Westall. We wish to thank Rosalind Chivas, the chief learner at SOF, and the entire staff for their tremendous commitment to the learners and community of SOF. We especially want to recognize the SOF educators who contributed greatly to this volume: Deleah Archer-Neal, Aruna Arjunan, Thomas Emerson, Thomas Gaffey, Kate Hayes, and Kate Reber. Their willingness to go above and beyond represents the essence of SOF. We would also like to thank the previous administrators and educators who have influenced this work. Their dedication can never be questioned and their contributions have been significant. A special thank you is extended to Ellen Savitz and Betty Lindley. Their continuous support of SOF and its vision give evidence to their passion and the strength of the school's foundation.

At Microsoft, we would like to recognize the leadership and support of Anthony Salcito, general manager of the U.S. Microsoft Education team. His willingness to support a project of this nature, his vision for this school, and his understanding of the challenges truly demonstrates Microsoft's commitment to education. We would also like to thank Linda Zecher, corporate vice president of Worldwide Public Sector, who from the beginning has always asked us to do what's best for students. We also wish to thank Stacey Rainey, who continues to champion and drive Microsoft's efforts at SOF, along with Tony Franklin. Their passion for the school and its kids are seen every day. And, finally, thank you to the Microsoft communications team led by Tonya Klause. Their efforts to tell this story have been remarkable.

We are indebted to the American Enterprise Institute, and especially to its president, Arthur Brooks, for his unflinching support of this research and for fostering an environment of collegiality and remarkable intellectual freedom. Finally, we would like to express gratitude to our publisher Doug Clayton at Harvard Education Press for the outstanding work he did in translating the manuscript into the book that you now read.

About the Editors

Mary Cullinane is director of innovation and business development for the Microsoft Corporation. A former teacher, she joined Microsoft in 2000, where she has worked to promote innovative programs and initiatives, including as national program manager of the Anytime Anywhere Learning Foundation and creator of the Microsoft Innovation Center Awards. In 2003, Cullinane accepted the position of School of the Future technology architect, in which she was responsible for driving the creation of the new high school. In 2008, she became the U.S. director of innovation and business development for the Microsoft Education Group. Cullinane, a recipient of the Microsoft Circle of Excellence Award, has spoken at national and international conferences on topics such as educational technology, school reform, and strategic leadership. She has testified before Congress and has appeared on PBS, National Public Radio, and ABC News, and in *Wired* magazine.

Frederick M. Hess is a resident scholar and director of education policy studies at American Enterprise Institute (AEI) and an executive editor of *Education Next*. His many books include *When Research Matters* (Harvard Education Press, 2008), *No Remedy Left Behind* (AEI Press, 2007), *Educational Entrepreneurship* (Harvard Education Press, 2006), *Tough Love for Schools* (AEI Press, 2006), *Common Sense School Reform* (Palgrave Macmillan, 2004), and *Spinning Wheels* (Brookings Institution Press, 1998). His work has appeared in both popular and scholarly outlets, including *Social*

Science Quarterly, the *Harvard Educational Review*, *Education Week*, *Phi Delta Kappan*, the *Washington Post*, and *National Review*. Hess serves on the review board for the Broad Prize in Urban Education, as a research associate with the Harvard University Program on Education Policy and Governance, and as a member of the research advisory board for the National Center for Educational Accountability. He is a former high school social studies teacher and has taught at Harvard University, Georgetown University, the University of Pennsylvania, and the University of Virginia.

About the Contributors

Deleah Archer-Neal is a special education educator and building representative for School of the Future in Philadelphia. She joined the SOF team prior to the school's opening in September 2006. As an advocate for eradicating labels and redefining special education, Mrs. Neal has worked with her teammates to create a full-inclusive model. Mrs. Neal's responsibilities include managing special education files and Individualized Education Programs, providing remediation and enrichment for learners with and without disabilities, coaching cheerleaders, and working with the 2010 curriculum-planning committee.

Aruna Arjunan is a math and social studies educator at School of the Future in Philadelphia. She joined SOF in the fall of 2006. Outside of the classroom, Ms. Arjunan has served on the curriculum-planning committee and the new educator orientation-planning committee. She has also has coached boys and girls tennis at SOF.

Jan Biros is associate vice president for instructional technology support and campus outreach at Drexel University. She joined Drexel in 1986 to market courseware developed by Drexel faculty as part of the microcomputer program established in 1983. Ms. Biros has been involved with the Philadelphia School District, the Mayor's Commission on Literacy, and Philadelphia Futures. She served on the advisory and development committee organized by

Microsoft and the School District of Philadelphia to create School of the Future, and was a member of the technology advisory committee for the Franklin Learning Center in Philadelphia.

Thomas Emerson is an English and social studies educator at School of the Future. In addition to teaching, he directs the school's annual musical and serves on the curriculum-planning committee. He earned degrees from Villanova University and the University of Pennsylvania. He has been teaching at SOF for two years.

Chester E. Finn Jr. is president of the Thomas B. Fordham Institute and a senior fellow at Stanford's Hoover Institution. During his career, Mr. Finn has served as a professor of education policy at Vanderbilt University, counsel to the U.S. ambassador to India, legislative director in the office of former senator Daniel Patrick Moynihan, and assistant secretary of education for research and improvement. He serves on the board of numerous organizations concerned with primary and secondary schooling, and has authored 14 books and over 350 articles. His work has appeared in *The Weekly Standard, Christian Science Monitor, Wall Street Journal, Washington Post, New York Times, Education Week, Harvard Business Review,* and the *Boston Globe.*

Thomas Gaffey has been a math and technology educator at School of the Future since 2007. He holds the position of technology teacher leader, a position in which he provides differentiated professional development of instructional technology for the faculty and staff. Mr. Gaffey is a member of the school curriculum-planning team and the school district's curriculum-articulation team. Before joining SOF, Mr. Gaffey attended Drexel University and Temple University.

Thomas Gift is a doctoral student in political science at Duke University. Previously, he was a research assistant in education policy studies at the American Enterprise Institute. Mr. Gift is a graduate of Washington and Lee University.

Michael Gottfried is a doctoral candidate in applied economics at the University of Pennsylvania's Wharton School of Business. He is also an Institute of Education Sciences pre-doctoral fellow and is on the board of editors of the *International Journal of Educational Advancement.* Mr. Gottfried earned his degrees from the University of Pennsylvania and Stanford University.

Margaret E. Goertz is codirector of the Consortium for Policy Research in Education and a professor of education policy in the Graduate School of Education at the University of Pennsylvania. Ms. Goertz previously taught at the Edward J. Bloustein School of Planning and Public Policy at Rutgers University, and was a senior research scientist and executive director of the Education Policy Research Division of the Educational Testing Service. She has published five books and more than three dozen chapters, articles, and monographs, including *School-Based Financing* (SAGE, 1999, coedited with A. Odden) and *From Cashbox to Classroom* (Teachers College Press, 1997, coauthored with W. Firestone and G. Natriello).

Kate Hayes is a counseling educator and the organizational chair for School of the Future. She has been a part of the project since the school opened in September 2006. Ms. Hayes's responsibilities include learner intervention, case management and programming, flexible school scheduling, project offerings, assessment presentation, and various university partnership programs. Before joining SOF, she was a graduate assistant in the Office of Student Life at Villanova University, where she collaborated on learning-community and service-learning projects.

Dorothea Lasky is a doctoral student in education at the University of Pennsylvania, where she studies creativity, educational policy, and twenty-first-century learning. She has done education research at Harvard's Project Zero, the Harvard Museum of Natural History, the Center for Arts Education, the Institute of Contemporary Art, and the Philadelphia Zoo. She is a graduate of Harvard University, the University of Massachusetts Amherst, and Washington University. She is the author of two books of poetry, *AWE* (Wave Books, 2007) and *Black Life* (Wave Books, 2010), and several chapbooks. Her poems have appeared in nationally recognized literary journals, including *American Poetry Review, Boston Review, The Laurel Review,* and *Columbia Poetry Review.*

Doug Lynch is the vice dean of the Graduate School of Education at the University of Pennsylvania, where he teaches courses on corporate learning, the economics of education, and social entrepreneurship. He worked previously at New York University, where he led numerous online learning initiatives, at the College Board, and at Arizona State University, where he helped launch one of the country's first charter schools. Mr. Lynch is chair of the U.S. delegation to the International Standards Committee project on global standards in nonformal education. He is the coauthor of *Corporate/ Higher Education Partnerships.*

Kabeera McCorkle is a doctoral candidate in reading, writing, and literacy at the University of Pennsylvania's Graduate School of Education.

Patrick McGuinn is an assistant professor of political science at Drew University. His work on education policy has been published in popular and scholarly journals, such as *Publius: The Journal of Federalism, The Public Interest, Teachers College Record, Educational Policy,* and *Journal of Policy History.* He has also contributed chapters to the edited volumes *Educational Entrepreneurship* and *No Remedy Left Behind.* His first book, *No Child Left Behind and the Transformation of Federal Education Policy, 1965–2005* (University of Kansas Press, 2006), was honored as a *Choice* outstanding academic title. Mr. McGuinn is a former high school teacher.

Dale Mezzacappa has reported on education since 1986, most of that time with the *Philadelphia Inquirer.* Before taking over the education beat, she was in the Trenton and Washington bureaus covering politics and government. Her work has won several local and national journalism awards, including for a series spanning thirteen years that followed 112 inner-city sixth graders who were promised a free college education by a wealthy philanthropist. Ms. Mezzacappa is currently a contributing editor at *The Philadelphia Public School Notebook*, a quarterly independent and nonprofit publication. She also teaches a journalism course at Swarthmore College and sits on the board of the Education Writers Association.

Kate Reber is an English and social studies educator at School of the Future. Since joining SOF in fall 2007, she has taught English and social studies, psychology, theater production, and other courses to first-, second-, and third-year learners. Outside of the classroom, Ms. Reber has served on the curriculum-development and orientation-planning committees, and in 2009 she oversaw the site-selection process for twelve new SOF educators. Ms. Reber earned degrees from Columbia University and the University of Pennsylvania.

Matthew Riggan is a researcher at the Consortium for Policy Research in Education at the University of Pennsylvania. His work has appeared in the edited volume, *The Implementation Gap: Understanding Reform in High Schools* (Teachers College Press, 2008), and is forthcoming in the *Peabody Journal of Education*. His current evaluation work includes studies of the Annenberg Foundation's Distributed Leadership Initiative and the William Penn Foundation's Twenty-First-Century Skills Project. He teaches research methods at the University of Pennsylvania's Graduate School of Education and the Wharton School of Business.

Index